Beaten Up Beaten Down

A. Razor

Punk ✪ *Hostage* ✪ *Press*

Beaten Up Beaten Down
A. Razor

ISBN 978-0-9851293-4-7

Punk Hostage Press
P.O. Box 1869
Hollywood, CA 90078
www.punkhostagepress.com

Editor: Antonio Maranzano

Introduction: S.A. Griffin

Cover Design: Geoff Melville

Author Photo: Los Angeles Police Dept.

Editor's Acknowledgements

This is a work of love, as broken and as bruised as love can be when it has been dragged over the terrain that these words navigate.

This is also a work of hope, as much as one can find hope in hopeless moments or borrow it from somewhere or someone else when the well of hope has been vanquished.

This is a work that reflects the culture of desperate living when the pursuit of material is muted by the pursuit of the muse, the voice it inspires and a renewal of that voice when it becomes depleted by hard living and even harder circumstance.

In essence, this a book of celebration. The reason for which is much more than the mere survival of ill fated dreams, but a strength in what is discovered on the journey of pursuit for those dreams.

The goal orienteering of a madman, some might say, if they were so inclined as to wonder what reservoir such pursuits might emanate from.

There are countless sources of support for this journey that this writer has walked. Most notably the writer's partnership with Iris Berry in founding Punk Hostage Press in order to give a platform for this presentation. Also notable is the participation of all those who have taken part in the inception of Punk Hostage Press into a conduit for many voices of contemporary literature and an opportunity to disseminate these tomes to an audience of like minded and actively creative folks.

People like Luis J. Rodriguez, Naima Steiner, Lee McGrevin, Amy Watson, Geoff Melville, Bucky Sinister, Danny Baker, Lisa Cherry, S.A. Griffin, Doug Knott, Joe and Kim Dalessandro, Jack Varnell, Diana Rose, Richard Modiano, Rafael and Melissa Alvarado, Billy Burgos, Hugo Muchaca, Nicholas Sanchez, Cyrus Amini, Michele McDannold, Murphy Clamrod, Edaurdo Jones, Jack Shaw, Bill Gainer, Puma Perl, Will Lopas and his family, Deana Privott and her family, Felix A. Montague and his family, Kaki Marshall, Presh Jewels, Uncle Hambone, Rick Lupert, Laurel Ann Bogen, Susan Hayden, boona cheema, Dannyboy Smith, Benjamin Rew, Jenna Kacy, Kenneth Rains Shiffrin, Jeff Jampol, Candi V. Auchterlonie, Frank Reardon, April M. Bratten, Jason Hardung, Jennifer Joseph, Jon Longhi, Jennifer Blowdryer, Chris Davis, Michael Marcus, Mj Taylor, Rachel Winner, Geoff Moore, Sevie Bates, Steve Perilloux, M. Chef Roussel, Paddy Mack, Steve and Tracy Wilkins, Kerry Marcus, JJ Cortez, Dennis and Annette Cruz, Corrie Greathouse, Rich Ferguson, J de Salvo, Carolyn Srygley-Moore, Paul Corman-Roberts, John Dorsey, Rob Plath, Dire McCain, Blaire Borkowski, Louisa Pillot, Quiet Mike, Chupacabra, Gabrielle Z. Falzone, David Maldonado, Kobie Grimes, Hannah Wehr, Forest Simon, Terence Lundy, Emilie Sciarli, David West, Maureen McNally, Meagan Murphy, Shira Tarrant, Phd, Kelly Gray, Michael Juliani, Ben de La Torre and Christopher Deinstag.

Without these folks, and many more, this book would have never been in your hands now, ready to read and pass on in hopeful inspiration to live a life full of renewal at every opportunity. – A.M. 2012

Introduction

We're all talkers, storytellers, that's what we do. Some abstract salvation amidst our raging humanity and flighty imaginings, some vague affirmation of what is truth, what is real, when of course there is no truth or reality at all except whatever we can glean from the same river twice. This is where stories come from. Not the past, not really, because that, like the future, simply will never exist, but from the present that we are always attempting to find right in front of us, the be here now. Stories are sensual beings, living things received via the senses then sent special delivery to the heart, then on to the most relevant facsimile of truth we can manage whether it is manifest from the throat, via the page or sent streaming headlong without thought or apology via digital media. I learned storytelling from the talkers. All those older people, whoever they were. All those wild eyed eccentrics, the strangers that make a life, anyone that would talk, tell a story as together we became great birds of a fractured feather. I was born into beat culture and I never knew it until I more or less rediscovered it in my 20s, for I too in my own way, and with my own unique history in tow, am not unlike the hero of this book; *Beaten Up Beaten Down*.

Much is made of Beat culture past and present. I am often accused of being "beat", which I immediately deny. That was some other time, I tell them, some other angry young man, not me. Yes, I have deliberately followed a path, searched out it's authors, artists, philosophers and been informed by the music. Broke bread, been on the road with, partied with and exchanged ideas with some of the progenitors and torchbearers of the scene. I was once lucky enough to spend an afternoon with Allen Ginsberg. I was tasked to squire him about Los Angeles in my old '59 Cadillac, taking him here and there, and ultimately getting him to LAX on time to get along to his next destination. This was the late 80s and you could still hang with somebody at the airport while they awaited their flight. We spent three hours together talking over tea and chocolate cake, discussing what was poetry. The conclusion was that poetry is candor.

For myself the Beat Generation continues to remain relevant, and of course this completely depends upon how you view it and how you use it, how you define yourself and how you allow yourself to be defined. I believe that yes, in regards to the original issue, the true progenitors of whatever and whoever it was, is much the same way that many of us that were there view punk: it is long time passing. And even at that, was it ever? Mostly these movements are peopled by very few true leaders, very few visionaries, most movements are populated by fashionmongers, which is true of what might be called the Beat Generation and the subsequent legions that have followed for more than 50 years now, myself included. When curiosity seekers, young hipsters and those stumbling thru the process come my way, I tell them all the same, as much as it might appear so, I am not interested, nor am I consciously practicing any sort of nostalgia. I bow deeply and give a generous tip of the hat to the past, hope for the future, but do my very best to live in the present, which is at best, an idea. I have been schooled by some of the best and I carry them with me, all of them, everyday, as they still inform me. I have been unbelievably lucky in that my friends have all been my greatest teachers, and my teachers my greatest friends and allies. What I have gleaned from all that I have read and experienced of things beat is exactly that, deal with what is directly in front of you, the process. Nothing else maters, and if you know me at all, you will hear me speak of this often as this is my guiding light that illumes all things.

Beat might be a world of inclusion, a world of moments, of lost fathers. A leaderless quorum of seekers with an insatiable need to know, poets and writers outside the margins, and not for any other reason except this is how they are and how it is. Like levy, covering the world with lines. As Kerouac himself spoke to it, beyond just beat from the street and Huncke's Times Square hustle, but beatific from the heart, in practice and spirit. The indefinable, unutterable IT, and you'll know when you get there, if ever. An imperfect search for an impossible perfection as a series of moments we call living; an epic howl, a magnificent journey and words without end. Crazy all night dancing, hungry wheels directed by hungry minds on the road to who knows where.

Beaten Up Beaten Down, all these things I find in my friend A. Razor. I have known him for many years. We crawled around the clubs together back in the good old bad old days of black leather rage against the machine. But I have really only become close to him as a friend and colleague since reconnecting with him during this past decade. Tough as nails with a bluebird in his heart that he can never drown, he is one of the most well read individuals I have ever met. But text and a facile memory alone won't cut it, you must have experience, creative gift and the ability to lay it down in order to approach the craft of writing, to be a poet. I have watched he and his work grow and I can tell you for a fact, he is process all the way. He and his work are one in the same, trying to tell his story as he falls along his own unique journey. I have watched him evolve as he has become a great poet and storyteller, one of the best of the genre.

We are storytellers, unique in experience, one to the other and on to the next. Most of us, whether we like it or not, widgets on the corporate chain gang, miners working for the company store, children of the bomb, slaves to technology and all the other ologies that we have allowed to define us when we, if we are to be beat and beaten at all, quite possibly should be worshipping the moment and all that is in it. First thought, best thought... are words and worlds holy? Is the moment holy? Is holy holy?

We are at a seminal place in our history, in our letters, existing within a world of unprecedented flux and discovery. We take what we can from the past, real and/or imagined, and we do our best to move forward and not live rearview. Move forward not as imaginary outlaws spinning bullshit with a pen like some western fantasy, but again as writers, artists, musicians, thinkers movers and shakers outside the margins by need, as acts of candor in process.

I do not pretend to know what beat is really, or beaten, I only know what I know and that is all, and it is absolutely true, the older you get, the less you know. But I can tell you this, *Beaten Up Beaten Down*, A. Razor has lived it and loved it, as is evident in this book. Go for the ride, embrace the mystery, dig the scenery and the characters that color the journey, then you tell me.

S.A. Griffin

Los Angeles CA

November 11, 2012

Dedication

This book is for all those who have been beaten, up or down. This book is also for the who get beaten still, from time to time. This book is for those who get the beat, the beating, the beatific, the awesome interconnectedness of all thing beating as one.

This book is for all those I have loved and cared for, many of whom loved and cared for me in return, who have been beaten up, been beaten down, but got back up as best they could, standing for what they ultimately believed in. This book is also for all of those who I only have memories left of that took those beatings alongside me. For all those who did not survive the beating, lost their beat or their way, and beat no more, except in the way they are still remembered and celebrated.

This book is for all the enemies and adversaries that thought they could beat me into some form of silence or submission. You made the way difficult, but you made the struggle more meaningful, because it is in transcending my desire to fight back against you personally then, and now only the ideas that you stood for, so that I might finally believe in justice again. The struggle that drives the beat in my heart is a part of my soul and my soul belongs to the community of the disenfranchised, marginalized voices that speak out, but are unheard for the most part due to the constantly beating drum of modern conformity. This is just to show that even after being beat down, or beat up, ideas that have heart and soul still matter, and I thank all those in my family, my friends, my community that helped wipe away the blood and start over, still beating back against what has beaten us all, never giving in to being beaten again. Never letting go of the beat, holding on to it, for dear life and for all it's worth, until getting beaten up and beaten down take the final toll.

It most assuredly will, as it always does, eventually.

Please, when it happens, don't forget to celebrate, not just for me, but for all those who I celebrate in these pages and more. The connections we have to each other truly are all that we have coming into or going out of this world. The memories of those connections are what make the process possible, even in the most beaten moments we will know.

A. Razor

Point Richmond CA

November 11, 2012

Contents

"I worked hard for this, I want you to know that."

- Al Pacino as Tony Montana in "Scarface"

*"It's too bad, somebody should've given it to you,
 you would be a nicer person."*

*- Michelle Pfieffer as Elvira Hancock in
                                "Scarface"*

On Whitman's Day

he was larger than life and never meant to come in a
sampler, but to be the dominate force he was
building an arsenal of flowers and trees among the
blades of grass that would march out into the world
on his behalf and permeate school children's books
lest their parents forget or maybe, never having
known, because ignorance is only bliss in the
moment you think you have it made in the shade
and the meteor is about to cleave your skull

there is no bliss beyond that metaphor so the
wildness will take you where it will until you read
and learn these words passed down, captain to
captain, as the years wear on the soles of weary
traveler's, at least the one's who have been given
cover for their feet, because long lines of words
have to be consumed, not traversed, and the more
you devour, the greater your sickness will be when
you lack them in your belly, so eat and feast along
the lines of pages sent down through the ages and
rejoice that this may be the closest form of salvation
you will know, to join in this celebration and be a
celebrity in the same moment as long as you
personify the stars in the sky and the woods and the
fields and the ocean's thunderous roar and the
desert sand's burning isolation and the fire that
burns scorched earth in battle and the stench of
bodies that have been bludgeoned for progress sake
and the rebuilding of cities after devastation and the
promise of a new world never fulfilled, but dreamed
in words that described the smallest organism and
spark of life to the greatest chasm of
misunderstanding the universe has ever imagined

and into the black hole of futures that would try to
sanitize the words and make them mean less than
advertising

behold this amazing journey that never ends, it rolls
down through time, because even the proclamations
of Alexander the great are less important than the
poems he wrote and no Grecian urn ever held
something as memorable as Homeric platitudes and
Shakespeare would have been a slavery auction
block barker if there had been no poetry and prose
to lighten the worst aspects of defeat and humiliate
the greatest accomplishments of a human race being
run full stride and reckless against gods who have
left us in the dust with their flying saucer chariots
many millennia ago

the smallest voice in all the universe that speaks of
microscopic yawps and is never heard beyond the
mulch at the edge of the pond and the debris at the
center of the largest trash heap in the world
tenement courtyard or out in the barren plains of a
dehydrated savannah or the jungles that hold the last
revolutionaries, it is heard in that moment that your
senses turn inward and you are able to stay your
desire to be all you can be and part of the master
plan, and read these words and those words and any
words and that indecipherable yawp, that micro
cosmic sound will become a deafening roar, a
thunderous sonic boom that you will remember
your life by as you ride the shock wave out past the
undiscovered planets of our solar system and into
the icy reaches of deep space until you come to the
place where it all began and you will see Walt
Whitman's grizzly beard and you will realize you
have made it home again with enough gas to make
it to the store and back before you bed down for the

night under a multicolored starry quilt and on top of
a fresh grown mattress of grassy leaves and listen to
the howl of the dogs on the blustery solar winds and
the moaning of the mating cats inside quasars and
hope you only get sleep with words in the dreams
and languages in the sounds, speak for ever to me,
old man, I will always want to listen

Fredo vs. Catullus

some light is gold
some light is silver
all light is magic
to magicians
only to be
illumination
to lovers

born for the last time here
born again maybe light years away
in some future galaxy of stars
that never saw this ray of light
until it gets there one day
measured in a different way

spiraling into the void like wheels of fate
stopping on the number chosen while
passing on the love that is frozen

the last part of the cycle is nearly completed
the turning key has almost undone the lock

where will you go as one door opens?
where will you go as one door closes?
where will you go?

the time is closing now
some sundials have
no moons to mock them

a bullet sinks into a lake
with flesh and blood in its wake

light years away into the creation of the next

born for the last time here
born again in the future of now
the dimension is never diminished
it is always recreated in the
next space and time
before you even
know it

Where Were You The Day Kennedy Was Shot?

in a womb
in Brooklyn
8 months
into it

mom had moved
to new york
from dallas
years before

they called her
"tex"
she was tall
she was loud
she filled a
room
like the
lone star
lady
from the
yellow rose
state

there were
not many
folks from
dallas
in brooklyn
back then

after it happened
she stood out
like a target

she was shunned
she was spit on
she was cursed
as the world
became
very cold
very lonely

even my father
became distant

no one knows
why
to this day

mom's old boss
jack ruby
shot oswald
in the belly
while I was still
in my mom's
womb
as people
watched
on new
television sets

I was born
a month later
on christmas day

a month
after the
birth
my pops

caught
a couple
of slugs
in the back
of his head

mom took me
up in her arms
to raise me in
sunny california
far from the snow
that fell at the corner
of flatbush and church
the day I was born

but, that question of
where were you the day
they shot the president dead?
that used to be significant
now it means less and less

many assassins
have plied their trade
since that day in dallas
many bullets
have cleaved hope
away from fate

many have fallen
many are never
remembered
anymore
at all
which makes me wonder, to myself
where will we all be when the next bullet flies?

If Only Angels Screamed Their Songs
(inspired by Anne Waldman)

I have never learned the proper way
to accept the blessing of the lord
so I walk about with angels upon
my humbled mass of shoulders

when the angels leave my shoulders
anne waldman rests there in their place
she whispers at first in a sweetness that is all sugar
words
then shouts down devils that would send the words
into anthills of damnation fire that spins them
into cotton candy dreams of slick city infernos

she gives instructions in clear breaths that
are more than suggestions as they are more
like newborn commandments to speak more
clearly about the will that dies in my blurred
eyesight as I lose her cadence into the night
of words that are crisp and sharp as they are
most likely hardened into a mantra of what I
need to say with an emphatic voice that says
yes to coming forth with truth and no to misled
sensations that have led an easier life than most
have known as I wonder aloud about an atheist
bomb that renders the last religious invocations
into meaningless pop songs that all the kids
load onto their playlists as they sleep on the
hopeful dream that the next vampire they meet
has their own cable episodic marketing strategy
in the works as anne screams so loud into my
ears that all activity is ceased and politics...
fucking politics
politics never really meant shit to me

as long as I had shoulders covered
with angel crap even though the
world called me a statue
loved by pigeon nations
with heads that bobble
up and down like little
pistons on little engines
that run into trouble
when the poisonous
most fastest of
all foods
is left out
overnight
for the imaginary saints

will the angels ever return ?
I would not want their presence
to make anne waldman
leave my side tonight
the mountains are
rocky
the way is treacherous
without her
melodic screams
to guide me

Desolation Angels Fall Too

do you lose your place
or your turn around here?

do you gain distance
or lose space over there?

between is where your thoughts
take you into a lush jungle of feelings
that come with their own sensations
coming to life in arcing sparks of
electrical charges across states and
boundaries and deep into walls of flesh
that quiver and part in aching acceptance
to the ghost of christmas future in a balled
up fist with only your natural juice flowing
over scarred knuckles for lubrication

a self oiled cylinder head on a hopped up
love machine with no handles and a fast ride
across the grassy plains and past the crack
of perky ass cheeks to hit home at the crux
of the matter where the spark burns into
the skin and leaves its mark on purpose
so that it never gets lost this way again

you stand for it
too long for pain
too long for pleasure
you stand for it
again and again
outside of a box
that was never
a set up or
even set up

your are only broken if you fall
you only fall if you love
you only quench if you
drink this overflowing manic
jism down your open throat
and let it soak your heart
with milky good warmth

you are only bent if you
lean into the wind as it
blows away thoughts
as it pushes passions
down sideways with the dirt
in a tango that tastes like rust
on a blood filled moon in
a december night's last
glimpse of steel inside
fragile wings of wax melting
away like a heart made of sand
as it pours out its
last hourglass
into the wind
that blows it
all alone

this angel may never come
but the destination your compass
has directed your soul to take
is going down like a falling
tree in a forgotten forest
that has grown so tired the
second it was born as a
lusty seed for pollen
looking for an up
escalator to the

gun store with
a trigger
that works
both ways

April's Submission

may your crossed fingers
                            secretly and softly
            break the legs
                        of editors
                                    who peruse them
forcing their choice into your palm
                        ...forcing their hand into your
submission...
may your crossed words not puzzle query
                        stop
                                    minds
                                                before
                                                hearts
may your finished product   be your
project*(tion)*
                                    into open territories of all
may your crossed legs uncross
    welcome your love home   words be damned
                                                words be done
    it's all hope from the heart

                                    here it is for you

Late Night With Uncle Bill's Last Word

there are no causes left to fight
that are not being fought
somewhere by someone
that you never met
but yet, you know them better
than you know your self
so you keep fighting
there will be more of it
after you die
even if you are already dead
and don't know it yet
fighting through the bardo
against the beast of your mind
against the creatures of your soul
against the monsters of your will
you will never have to surrender
it will eat you alive as much
as it will eat you dead
like old filthy mcnasty
wrenching on the eternal crankcase
of sisyphus old chopped hog
while old fast eddie keeps slipping out of sight
certainly he must be circling back around, always
dino died in mexico, just past san felipe
the shallow grave was really just a hiding place
berto takes too many magic bullets
shuffles off stage left to the coast
no applause from the underinformed audience
candy is a girl dressed like a woman
she turns blue in a dark blue motel room
cold and stiff as your love laying there
next to her in the morning
the last take in the scene before they yell cut
too many times down little starla's wrist

as she makes jello molds of her last moment
leaving you with one last cigarette
that the paramedic takes away as the cops
take you away, again, as usual
big paulie saw it coming so many times
you got to give it to him in the face
just so he knows what time it is
it can ruin the funeral
but nobody goes to those anymore, anyway
there are stories about how mona died
in your arms as they were swollen tired
and shot out for days
there are carloads and truckloads
of bad accidents on the road
none as sad as your little baby girl
crying down the shiny concrete halls
as you huddle with thorazine slippers
and lithium pajamas on the vacaville tier
plotting out the revenge of sharpened
tooth brushes shoved into eye sockets
before the guards can fire the first fatal
warning shots into the head of your worst friend
getting left alone to fight into the night
wake up with no sleep fighting, always
fighting still into the sun or the stormy outcome
walking with swagger staggering with false pride
you always want the first taste of anything
people tell you that you might have killed too many
you never kept count, can't pin nothing on em
except bad math in hard circumstances
as train tracks truck by into the long distance haul
bags & balloons & bottles & balls
all getting their kicks with you as tears run away
with the moon /with the stars/ with the sun /with it
all

even into the wild blue yonder into hells built for
two
until it is a lonely ticket, reserved for one
watch what's on the menu
the surgeon general said eating pussy causes
throat cancer more so than cigarettes
you quit smoking, among other things, but
don't be an afterlife pussy, don't stop living this one
even if they tell you that you are dead, keep going
use up all the oil, eat up all the corn, free all the
slaves
like it was you all along, come to save something
only it was you all along, that had something saved
something they couldn't take from you
something you held onto forever like a supernova
even after nicki hepatitis told you to never leave
which was fitting, so much so, that your last word
was LOVE
with no PEACE
without ever saying good bye

A Driving Distraction

dead wasp on the dashboard, looking up into
eternity
frozen in a death spiral, curled against a finality
a lost momentum of waspness earmarked by
six legs jutting upward, hinging backward
as if to say...
"I am no longer accountable
for my last stinger's transgression
or the consequences of my sting
I must decline into decomposition
to save the world from itself
or even merely, just to die
against a windshield of
a futile struggle with
an open window
looming nearby..."
the last words
of a hapless
wasp
come on
with a rapid
clarity unlike any
others I have known
at least for now, until
this traffic begins to move again

Time Lapse Photographic Memory

it felt like she went missing
without you ever knowing
got so lost, so far away
like she was never there
or never even here in the
here now and that's how
it happens when the dust
settles before the storm hits

it seemed like she was never
going to go anywhere without
saying goodbye one last time
like there was a connection that
couldn't be severed or broken
without the sounding of an alarm

it happened in silence with an extreme
close up of absence that did not make
hearts grow fonder but instead shrank
them with a fear that it had been a dream
with no waking moments to calculate the
next move and it never seemed sexy until
there was no sex and the ultimate realization
that there never had been unless it was done
with your own manipulation and the loudspeaker
quaked the floor as they called for a clean up on
aisle 6 where the textual emotions were held as
weakened prisoners in a concentration camp that
could not remember what came next in the
preamble
that was a audition for a part in a passion play about
a world with no gods, only actors & directors &
crews
& the scenic design held together with

nothing but
a gaffer's tape hope

it all came down like a house of cards
as blanketed diseases
overtook forsaken hearts that melted
in the battery acid of an
instant message promise that was bereft of
any feeling
having no intention of being the love you could
depend on
 in a winter storm   only to become
another love TKO on the way to the consolation
round that held the last attempt at contact like a
jealous child
 wields a razor blade
in a candy shop of horrors that keeps
 the longest run
 going on theater row
until the last curtain reveals the backstage is empty
 the hearts have all
left the building
 to join their families
 in the carnage of the catastrophe that
had claimed the loves of all the heartaches
that never had a chance to hurt

it was a floor missing on a tower that served a hot
pancake
 made of dust and flame
it was a flash of lightning across a skyline of
injustice
 that blinded the only witness
it was a wave that moved no liquid shape or audible
sound

toward a shoreless coast
it was a blindness that wakes up before you do, all
forlorn
 and tearful about nothing
it was a sodomy of an institution that took more
 than it wanted to give and gave less
than it wanted to take
 until there was nothing left to hide and only the
wisdom
 of the last
experience to share before the earth moved away
 from the foundation and revealed it
had better things to do than wait on her to get back
from
 god knows where to tell you
god only knows about god knows what
until she says, with bared teeth that are clenched so
tight,

"Get up off your god damned knees, already, I am
your atheist of love and agnostic of lust, you will
never worship this right here!"

while never forgotten,
this picture
would never be taken
again

hibbing

no longer any holy land
up on the iron range

no children left to sacrifice
they have left the wild plain

moving on into the big city
gone away to seek his fame

nobody does his killing
up on the iron range

the songs he steals
are real ones

the song he sings
so vain

the word was always
plentiful
in a world
of pain

but, the wind
it howls
so primitive
howling out
his name

he tires now
of hearing it

it always sounds
the same

Reading HOWL with S.A./Watching HOWL with Iris

Part 1

Old Man Red had given me the worn edged book and told me to read it on a rainy day on Hollywood Blvd.

It didn't seem like much at first, but he insisted this had the importance of any of the big books I was looking at that day.

I had just gotten my first room of my own in a run down house up in Laurel Canyon and it had bookshelves, bookshelves, bookshelves that begged to be filled and, lord knows, I wanted any women I brought in there to think of me as smart enough to be something other than what I felt inside, so I wanted to fill the bookshelves and Red was the man with the store that had cheap used books as well as expensive new ones. I figured I could make a deal with the old codger, since making little deals on the boulevard and down on the boardwalk or over in the canal had become quite a forte for me. Red was helpful and glad to see I had some money, but he insisted I take this little, old book with simple, bold letters across the front reading "H-O-W-L."

He said "This is the bible of the beatniks, it will help you understand your mother better." I remember that because Red knew me and my mom did not get along too well at the time and he knew my mom claimed to have been a "beatnik" or beat something, before I came into the world and after that it seemed to just be about beating me. I knew I had it coming most of the time, but still, every kid on Hollywood Blvd. had an axe to grind back then, and I ground down axes with the best of them. I didn't really get it when I read it. I took the book back a few days later on a mission to get some stuff that Bukowski had referenced in his Notes column. I tried to give the book back to Red, but he bristled. "Did you read the damn thing or not?"

I was a little taken aback. I had heard of this Ginsberg guy, from my "godmother", she was a hippie, toured with the Grateful Dead, gave me the best shrooms and acid, and read and wrote poetry that did not make a lot of sense to me. This seemed like more of that gibberish that she would make me listen to and I would oblige her because I was at her place in the canals of Venice to get some of that good stuff and to get a little money for some of my good stuff. It seemed like professional courtesy to listen to her recitation as we smoked a doobie and some Ravi Shankar played in the background. But this was, while interesting enough in its use of words that just a few years before would have made me giggle to read, making reference to something that I didn't quite get yet. Pussy was my god as a teenager, or goddess to be more gender specific, and the reason I wanted to read and be smarter was because I had stumbled into the world of attainable pussy in the dark bars and strange parties that I would slide into at night, pretending to be older than I was, and making plays at older women. Even though I read every day, voraciously, all the things that seemed important, poetry was still a bit mysterious to me. I was still struggling with Whitman, Frost, cummings, Pound, but totally enthralled with Poe and Kipling. I was dramatic enough, but not quite romantic enough. I had begun reading Bukowski, which was teaching me romance on terms and conditions that I could relate to, but I still read more of his prose than his poetry. I rarely wandered over to Western Ave. because that area was not as welcoming as the Hollywood I frequented. And, being a young boy/man when in I was in Venice, I would rather be in the water on a hot day than reading at the bookstores on the boardwalk. So the real poet in me had yet to emerge, but I knew I had give it a go the same way a kid knows he will get no pudding if he doesn't eat his veggies and meat, even if it is brussels sprout and chopped liver to him.

"All right, I will give it another go, but what is so important about this one anyway? It is cheap looking and thin, I am trying to impress the ladies, Red, this book don't look like it is gonna do much of that."

"Criminy, kid, that damn book was once banned, sold like contraband, they put the publisher on trial, it set a legal precedent at the time, so guys like me could peddle books to dumbshits like you without the cops busting in and taking us all in to the hoosegow. That poem is the voice crying out for recognition, for validation, for some company on a lonely night of terror. What dame wouldn't want to hold on tight for that ride? You might not be as good with the dames as you say if you can't pick up on that one."

I had been playing with writing my own stuff up until then. I would still show up to this English Lit. class during the week and the teacher, Mrs. Waldech, would cut me slack on my truancy rate if I would write original work, short story or poem, and write something every week. It seemed like an easy hustle and I enjoyed the feeling of getting over on the school by giving her something in exchange for leniency. She was more of an Ayn Rand contemporary, so I read *Atlas Shrugged* prose and wrote short stories that were based off of ideas I got from Steinbeck and London. It wasn't very genuine writing to my experience and truth, but it got me out of trouble. I had not really discovered my own voice yet. Looking back on it from here, Red was making a recommendation that he knew would only be helpful in that respect.

"Look, read these, then read the HOWL piece again." He handed me an old book that was titled *The Selected Poems of Langston Hughes* ."This will help you understand the rhythm of jazz in poetry. This will open up a whole new world of understanding. I forget how young you really are, if you are even that age, I wonder sometimes." Red was pretty perceptive. I told him I was 17, going on 18, but he new I had a fake ID and went into several of the area bars. I had been going back and forth between San Bernardino, Hollywood and Venice for a couple of years now. I was 15, going on 16, but I was wise for my years and motivated. I wanted to get this, to pull this off, to survive the crazy circumstances I had wandered into by being born and had been seemingly wandering into ever since.

"Thanks, Red, I'll read em up." I took the books, along with a Hemingway, Fitzgerald, Miller and Nin that I had purchased for the shelves, and went on my way. I was building my first library of books. I did not like school so much, but I loved reading. The fact that I was now living in a room that had once been a study was perfect for me. It was my refuge from all things Berdoo and street and unfriendly in my world.

I read the Hughes books and was so moved by the words and the movement of verse that I would imagine myself transported into those times of his struggle to be heard in the face of the racism and all the feelings he went through and poured into every line that reflected his experience and outlook. Red had gotten me. This was golden to me. I started to read less of Bukowski's prose and more of his poems. I read HOWL and I realized that it was meant to be read aloud. That people wrote these poems and read them aloud, screamed them, somewhere. I realized what my mother was doing in the Village in the 50's a little better. I started to open up in a way that was new and awesome.

Then a tragedy struck. A friend I had known my whole life was walking with me down a street in San Bernardino. We had gone to a "ditching" party. We had been drinking all afternoon and some fights had broken out when the kegs were dry, so we left to get some more beers and go to the park to drink them. We were laughing and buzzed when all of a sudden shots broke up the moment and I hit the ground. I was not hurt, but my friend was bleeding out. He died there in my arms, although they would not pronounce him dead until they got him to the hospital. I went out to my room in Hollywood and stayed in it for a couple of days. I began writing in a way I had never written before. Two years later I would read Ginsberg's *Kaddish* and I would cry in the bookstore after reading it. My experience with HOWL had been potent and was compounded by what would quickly begin to happen around me.

45

The murder, the suicide, the insanity, the disease...it was all there in that poem, in long form, the way it drops along into your life. Just as present, as well, was the hope, the spiritual connection to survival, the celebration of the now in the moment it is read aloud.

Part 2

Ginsberg was an aging hippie throwback guru to me when I met him at the Naropa Institute many years ago. I was driving from New York City and back to San Francisco and I had an old girlfriend who was living in Boulder, Colorado that said I could kick some dust off there for a moment. I had done a few readings on my trip, the Nuyorican in the LES, an artists loft in Williamsburg, a bar in Buffalo, a school in Rochester, a bar in Detroit, MI, an art gallery in Minneapolis, MN, a school in Iowa. I only had a few chapbooks left from the 300 I started out with. The books themselves only brought throw away money, I had paid for the gas and made enough cash by selling some speed, LSD and some weed long the way. Occasionally taking it with people who were putting me up and trying to be grateful as I could, because I was a fugitive in 3 states at the time, so housing me could be trouble for folks.

There was a reading at a cafe next to the Institute and my girlfriend was going to it the night I arrived. I was a little road weary, but I figured I could maybe read something if I felt compelled and sell a couple of the 2 dollar chapbooks and retire back to her place with some folks and party it up. She had a nice backyard with an old wooden hot tub and I was ready for some time off driving. The reading was cool, I learned about the Buddhist foundation of the school, sold some books, sold some acid, met a couple of real nice students from there that came back to the house and dropped acid and frolicked around naked all night. The next afternoon they took me to Naropa and showed me around. I was introduced to Ginsberg and we chatted briefly about some people we had in common. He told me to come and see him do a reading with musical accompaniment later that week as a guest. It seemed cool, but there had been these remarks and this letter that Ginsberg had written where he came out as a member of NAMBLA, or at least in support of them. I don't go throwing rocks much in my glass house, but that bothered me some. I was not at the least bit concerned with people's sexual freedoms as adults, I figured everyone needed love, or whatever, but my personal experience with the adult to child power differential was hard to mitigate with Ginsberg's revelation.

I had been out on the street a lot as a kid and had a seen the dynamic of teens being considered valuable chattel in the sex trades. I had experienced it first hand as three different girlfriends who had worked the streets died from suicide, overdose and at the hands of killer. All were under the legal age and felt the pressure, same as I felt, that you had something valuable to older people with money and you needed to cash in that value now, before it was too late. The too late was in reference to the fact that they were obsessed with your youth and it would be too late for them if you waited any longer. I didn't think of Allen in that way, as a predator, but

I didn't want to condone behavior that I really felt strongly about due to personal experience and not because of some sexual orientation prejudice that I didn't want to be a part of either. I was going to have to think hard about it so I could get to the truth for myself.

I was having a good time in Boulder, so I figured I might as well let the jets cool longer and catch the show. I just wanted to get clear on my feelings and I always felt a little vulnerable when coming down off of tripping. I talked with one of the girls that took a class from Allen in New York and had then come out here. She was really opened up to the whole chanting thing and the Buddhist spiritual aspect. I was willing to let go of my feelings to have the experience while I was there as long as I was honest about how I felt. She said she understood and we bonded for the next couple of days, writing haiku, drinking wine, smoking grass, reading Basho, Snyder, Alpert and Brautigan. I even left the speed alone, which was more because I needed what I had left for the rest of the drive. I sold out of the LSD and bought some decent homegrown mountain weed that kept me happy, too.

The reading was kind of strange at first, a lot of chanting to purify the room and whatnot, then some music from a sparse rhythm section and a dobro player. Allen read some stuff that resonated and some other wordings I did not connect entirely with, but I was stoned enough where I just went with it and latched on to what I liked and let go of what didn't work for me. It was easy enough. At the end, he announced that he would read HOWL, which he said he had not read out in some time. I

remembered my first copy of it and how, after
learning more about the trial and other writers and
the reading at Gallery 6, I had made it a point, on
my first trip to San Francisco, to purchase a copy at
City Lights and ask Ferlinghetti to sign it later.
Hearing the old man read it that evening was very
moving. It brought the piece alive in his voice and
you could see him get young again, get a hold of the
youthful exuberance that he wrote the piece with,
the feelings that this was it in every word. I really
knew Moloch after that reading. Really felt it as a
presence brought to life and dimension in those
words. my feelings about the poem changed again. I
rode on back to Frisco with a little different take on
being a writer.

Part 3

S.A. Griffin has graced the room at many readings
in my time. He has always been a pivotal part of the
world of writing in so many ways I can honestly say
I don't know anyone, especially in Los Angeles,
who adds to the culture of the written and spoken
word with as much effort and willing sacrifice to
create not only his own art, but to share it by
creating a community for it to be shared in and
encouraging others to stand as peers with him in
this community that, as he tells it, is a handed down
tradition that came from scared humanoids huddling
around campfires many millenia ago and now we
are in the moment with it now. There are plenty of
others who do a lot as well, but S.A. is just this time
proven entity for me and I have yet to meet anyone
who is worth their weight in ink that doesn't know

him or does not want to meet him. He has that
beatific shine when he wrangles the words around
and he has the consummate soul of a bard. He
seizes the moment and wrests all the feelings and
experience out of it while sharing it with anyone
willing to drop their inhibitions about flying freely
into words and sounds and join him. It is that spirit
that the beats had gotten from their influences and
wanted to pass on that Ginsberg had captured in
HOWL that I felt S.A. has always passed on to me.

When Rafael Alvarado called me recently to ask me
if I would participate in a reading of HOWL that he
and S.A. were putting on and I was like "When is it,
where do you want me to be?" as soon as I gave it a
minute to sink in. I am not a big "scene" guy. It is
just not my thing, I got outside issues and life
situations that I am involved in my whole life that
preclude any involvement on a serious level with
being in one place for readings on a weekly basis,
or submitting in to zines and publications and
making friends with people outside my inner circle
of people that I have come to trust with my life. The
last few years I have been changing that about
myself, but it made it so, as far as literary
connections that made me a part of anything, well, I
was pretty much the opposite of S.A. I was very
inconsistent, not really interested in sacrificing time
that I wanted to use doing other things and not
really seeing myself as a writer the same way a lot
of these other people did. So, now that I am trying
to do things differently than before, I am more
willing to try to participate and I am grateful when I
am asked to participate and try to minimize any
egocentric internal voice that would interfere with
me showing up and having a good time at an event

like this. I don't get loaded anymore, so the option to self-medicate is off the table, which means I got to show up and deal with these uncomfortable social situations that these events can be for me and just try to do my best.

Once again, I am not a performance poet, don't memorize stuff well at all, don't have the drive to deliver a performance for you; all I have that has ever worked for me is the desire to express my feelings in the moment I wrote something and transcend it into the feelings I am experiencing when I read it. It is kind of like a crude form of method acting, at best, but I am very comfortable at my rate of growth in this department over the years. I feel I possess a certain amount of integrity because I keep my experience doing spoken word true to who I was all those years ago when I got drunk and rambled out some punk rock lyrics off a crumpled piece of paper in the misguided hopes to have sex with a girl that had encouraged me to do so. I didn't get the pussy, but I got exposed to a whole world that I would dance around the periphery of for the next 30 years. I don't ever want to sell that experience short by forcing my reading at an audience. I have to just deliver it from my heart without my head getting involved too much.

Long story short, I said yes, S.A. made a poster, I saw who would also be at the reading, and I was very excited to be a part of it. I borrowed a book from Shira Tarrant, that was a complete HOWL, with notes and copies of original drafts, history of the poem and all the players in the trial with synopsis of the trial proceedings. I brought my friends Beah and Issa, who had never seen HOWL read out loud before. We got to the Sunset Laemelle 5, not far from where I had holed up over 30 years ago to read HOWL for the first time and begin to have an experience with all the different poetics I would encounter in life since then.

The reading began with Laurel Ann Bogen, who has been an important part of the literary movement in Los Angeles and world wide in one of the most consistent and concrete ways I have seen. Both her and Wanda Coleman were at the first readings I ever went to and I always learn something from her. After her lead , the reading was handed off from poet to poet like a hot potato or a relay baton, sometimes being read in choruses from both sides of the group, people coming in and out of it with S.A. punctuating moments giving everything he had to give. We howled and howled. Doug Knott, who was the M.C. at the first reading I went to in Silver Lake at the Lhasa Club and later at the VAC and the Onyx. Rafael Alvarado who also helped in setting up the event, Lorraine Perrotta, Steve Abee, Mende Smith, Brendan Constantine, Richard Modiano, Luivette Resto, Billy Burgos, Mike M. Mollett and a host of others that joined in and rode the thing like a wild cyclone until the end. No mics, no egos, no breaks or waiting, just full tilt boogie until it was done and it was holyholyholyholyholyholy.

It was a very humbling experience for me. Never thought I could make it this far. Never was looking to be a writer or a poet as much as I wanted to have something that was not corrupted in the face of all of the corruption that was in the world, that was in me. I have come to see writing as my spiritual connection to the inner and outer worlds that I live in. It has been a huge part of what has saved my life, guiding me through the darkest moments of insanity, despair, grief, loss, institutionalization, homelessness, hunger, addiction and pain. I think Ginsberg spoke to all of these in the most capable way he knew how to. He wove love through it as a common thread, an unconditional love that spread across everything, no matter what. A powerful statement, then and now, still very much relative to the world around us, and very much so to me on a personal level. When it was done, I went and watched the movie with Beah and Isabel. They seemed to really enjoy it, they are very enlightened girls to say the least. I went to sleep that night having a new experience with the poem HOWL and with all of the words of the world and the life I live by them. My integrity has never meant more or felt better since that day a couple of weeks ago.

Part 4

Iris Berry is the girl of my dreams, so to speak. We were introduced once backstage at The Scream Club, by Dayle Gloria's friend, who played in a band called Samman and The Apes at the time. She was pretty busy that night, but was cordial and kind. I was back there doing some business, but I told myself, one day I got to try to talk to her away from this scene. I was very taken by her. That was about 25 years ago, and that moment never came when I had hoped for it to, but in the last 5 years we have become close and dear friends. She was unable to make it to the reading that night and I told her what

I thought of the film and the experience. She wanted to see HOWL and I told her I would gladly go see it with her. We do a lot of stuff together lately, so it just seemed like a good idea without much thought going into it. Iris is editing my poetry manuscript for Luis Rodriguez's Tia Chucha Press, my first book published since the last of my chapbooks that was done over 15 years ago. She is the most perfect editor for this manuscript and Luis is the perfect publisher, it just doesn't get any better for a schmuck like me than that, even though it has been a long, hard time coming, it is so worth it now. I am proud to say that Iris and myself are connected by years of history and a common bond that is very special to me.

We met at Greenblatt's Deli for a turkey pastrami sandwich and a greek salad. As we sat down, Ron Jeremy came in and said hello to us as he walked to his table. We both knew the "hedgehog" from different scenes and encounters, but he we were crossing paths in Greenblatt's all these years later, which was the funniest, serendipitous moment for us right then. It was a pretty upbeat happy time and we kept it up all the way over to the theater across Sunset Blvd. The theater was near empty and we grabbed good seats and the film began. It was more emotional for me this time. I was more clear on the message and the portrayal of Ginsberg in the moment, with everything suspended in midair as the trial went on and he tried to explain to an interviewer what it was all about. The lines come from Ginsberg's own words and James Franco delivers them with a lot of authenticity. The whole film is shot and edited in a way that is indicative that it was very much a labor of love. It touched us

54

both in personal ways. We teared up, we laughed, we were in love with the moment that was on the screen. I don't have the ability very often to be very open like I was, and it was nice to feel safe enough to enjoy the film this way.

Since then I have spoken to some who did not enjoy the film when they saw it. I have spoken to others who did not see it, but don't like HOWL or Ginsberg or poetry or films or, for whatever reason, just did not like it or the idea of it. I know that it is valid that this occurs with art. No art is everyone's cup of tea. Art, in any form, is flawed in some aspect as it is created by the human experience as run though the artist and it is, therefor, human itself, somewhat. No one is right or wrong in this sense, no matter how strongly they feel they are, they can only be right in the sense that it feels that way for them personally and then they can align themselves with like-minded people and create their own or anti movement to what they feel so strongly about or against. After giving it thought and encountering several negative responses, I wrote a comment on Iris's page that stated thus-
.
"...I had an awesome time watching that film...it is inspiring to me...to think in terms of inclusion as opposed to exclusion...to see a literary movement begin in such a humble way...basically with a lot of love and not much else...it is doubtful.... there would have been the focus on that literary movement if not for the trial that ensued around the publication of howl, but also what made it important to the people portrayed in the poem, the reading at Gallery 6 in San Francisco that was hyped immediately and talked about and the

language passed on in an age with no internet or intricate personal phone service...these people became a community around this poem...this poem galvanized a consciousness that inspired people to have more readings, write more poems from the heart, help friends get published, hold readings in small, independent places, think differently about their place in the world, about their voice in the world...it shook the foundations of an academic stranglehold on the words that describe everyday people who strive toward a higher understanding of life in all its tragedies and love in all its glories...it set a permanent mark that has only been added to, even by people that dislike the poem, or the writer, or the publisher...it doesn't really matter, because if you get up in a room of people with a piece of paper to read your words out loud to them, to share your truthful bond to your muse, you are part and parcel of this...you are in its legacy, its tradition, its lineage, its canon...it is just a movie about a moment, or several moments, that combined, led to a discovery of self-truth for a writer (the reason I write myself) and the discovery of a hidden potential for a marginal group of artists that had never had access to the world beyond this precedence in such a way as to incite riots of base emotions that had been, prior to this howl, truncated into nothing that was permanent enough to notice or pass on so easily from generation to generation...I hope it is never lost into the dark margins again...I hope the howl will last forever..."

I stand by the comment and the sentiment in it. I have no squabble with anyone who believes contrary. I am very secure in my integrity and honesty regarding my art and my lifetime of work

56

in it. In the end, it is just a film, just a poem, just another writer beatified by accolades from sycophants. I don't really mean to add to that here. Just to memorialize the effect on myself and the people I have loved, the people I have lost, the people that have come and gone and those that stand by me today.

My people.

I have a lot of love for you all and it has something to do with these words that I write, whether I am right or wrong, under any opinions or circumstances.

Soul

ignorance walks alone at night in the jungle
  like a tiger
anger is no place to hide from the timing
  of right now
sections of self get peeled away against
  the resistance
like jaggedness to the blind on illuminated
  pathways

in the classification of souls
there are many kinds of holy

holiness is hardly understood by the wholly mind of
holy people

all souls rooted in the sojourn rule eternal
  as if immortal
those that are held by time
  are nine fold
  into nothingness
those that have stood at rest upon repentance
  are six fold
as such with no window
  into redemption
  but not forsaken

those souls that have self-originated possess
  an utterance
of the ineffable truth

(an utterance) existing only in relation
  to the power
  of eternal
life and light

there are four types of these souls

the first are as angels on high
supporting light from below
backs arching against the
weight of life as it is
lived among us

the second are those that love truth
they seek it no matter what
the balance or consequence

the third are those that love hope
until all ends, bitter or sweet
in the face of all dangers
against all odds

the lastly, not least
are those that simply believe *in this*
 illuminations originating from within
are incapable of not being connected
to those that are illuminated throughout
the expanding universal explosion
with the ultimate faith of life never ending
that in every explosion there *is creation*
in every death there *is life*
regardless
of the death of every life
or the birth of every light
for it has a radiance
in all its agreements
that can never be hidden
never be captured
never even be taken
for granted

or overtaken by fear
it is peaceful forever
inside you with wisdom

even tigers change direction
as it approaches them
through the jungle at night

it cannot be trapped for its brightness
from darkness it will always break free

Incestuous Calliope Block

spirits get sacrificed in effigy
atop skyscrapers below lights
on helicopters
around here eggs are frozen
into solid embryonic arguments
that dissolve in high alkaline water levels
lives are changed like smelly diapers that ooze
the sensual fecundity of lost seasons abroad
shares have gone down the tubes into the abyss
across the wasteland then through the wringer
guesses have been taken on which way the last act
of disappearing is seen to be headed for
scenes get twisted back around onto the freeway off-ramps
 before their last exit is required
fractals are segregated by impulses that leave
no tern unstoned
until nothing comes of it
memories are the stuff dreams are multiplied by
or divided into long enough to get a fraction
of the cost of tea in china that is bound for budapest
on the holy roller coaster of fruity delights
dropped down our throats that give lodging
to bad behaviors known to augment traditional learning
 into blank tirades of wisdomless retribution
for crimes against insanity
until probation
periods are extended into imperfect sentencing guidelines
 that restrict all movement that
precludes the extinguished parts of the brightest signal
 that turns corners into basket cases
full of magnified desires under microscopic emotional
states
 of ecstatic fearfulness that
shows its spiny head dress to the foot soldiers

on display against the border guards of some
unknown empire of delighted treasures that are preoccupied
 with the stranger formatting
of burned out genitals
 that no creature could find comfort in
on even the coldest of days

bottom line, this gets the damn job done
 because there was never anything that could top it
even in the quietest of corners
 or the loudest of harmonic divides

Rupali
for Pali

in a second womb of suffering
you were birthed to a second mother
with blessed Teresa of Calcutta
standing by as the midwife
guiding you toward a new life
in a big apple of a city
so far from the slums
you were abandoned into

you were determined and unhinged
leaving behind the comfort you were given
to stretch your vocal cords of angst
screaming down the streets and alleyways
all around the lower east side
drinking furiously down the alcohol
listening to the music loud as you could
screaming so loud the tent encampments
in Tompkins Square
never slept soundly
as you claimed the corners around
alphabet city
as your own against the cold
or all night without sleep
in the hottest august heat

you traveled out into the world beyond the bridges
to many cities of mini apples of golden gates
on bridges that you felt captured by
restless as a drunken nun you disrupted
the woman's shelter long enough
to get a night's sleep before you
returned to your Manhattan home
the movement tried to save you

but you were already moving
as fast as you could
the darkness was moving faster

like a wild tigress fighting for a place in a lonely
jungle
you ran and slashed and roared aloud
liquid in bottles failed you
pills in bottles failed you
powder on mirrors failed you
hope against hope failed you
love falling down into ash valentine cards
failed you broken hearted as you
felt more than you could handle

I missed my flight to the city of lost wages
drug away in chains and violence
as you waited for my arrival on the
saturated casino floor that we never saw together
I saw you last in Bolinas as my fate engulfed me
we angrily said good bye in an argument
as I never would drink with you again
because I would not drink with you that day
you flew back to New York City
to be left for dead on the hospital doorstep
like the orphan of Calcutta that you were born as
into this life with a starvation that was finally
not a hunger any longer
you left this world the day I went back to prison
your grieving mother
pulled you off of life support the night before
as I contemplated fate as a punishment
and punk rock music has never
sounded the same
since that day
and New York City doesn't scream

like it used to
for me
anymore

She Always Dreams Of Joan
for Louisahhh

she heard the music of unseen spheres
she heard the voices of unseen angels
her passionate simple words & songs
brought forth an armed resistance
to the deceit & corruption of tyrannical powers
unchecked by the hand
of any god almighty
she ran into the jaws of death headfirst
she ran into the crowns that lorded over her
as they clamped down
with their steely jaws of fearful vengeance
and the saint,
     who bent her sword toward the heavens
before she thrust it
into the devil's heart,
would burn,
for all of this,
for all of us,
for all time,
in flames that danced higher
than the highest cathedral spires
in smoke that blew across battlefields forever more
in smoke that brought real tears to the eyes
                    of angry warriors
felled by the swords of majestic deceptions
 that betrayed
all the love in their hearts
               all the life in their spirits

        these flames cool their tempers

these flames warm their souls

this is the fire she gave us
              to keep the cold from
           our lonely dying

                       ___hearts

sparky and I have a heart to heart
for Scott Wannberg (and Sparky, too)

"you always try to be so stoic when people are
lookin', mr. razor, don't you?"

"look, sparky, old boy, I am just trying to be strong
for you,
I figure scott would want it that way."

"I am not as old as you, old boy, and I call em like I
see em, tough guy, so
if you gotta let it out, just let it out, is all I'm sayin',
mr. razor."

"(sniff), really, it's just a head cold sparky...and
please, not so formal,
razor is just fine."

"well, scott always said you were a lil' tightly
wound...a lil' edgy, if you will..."

"all right, sparky, call me whatever the fuck you
want...jeez...you know, I like dogs,
more than I like people...I was a raised in a
kennel...out in berdoo...so you can drop
the passive-aggressive thing...I probably talked
more to dogs than people, if you
time it out...in my lifetime, I mean..."

"in a kennel? what on earth could those dogs have
done to deserve that kind of treatment?"

"well, I was...huh? nevermind...I just wanted to be
supportive...you know...throw a stick if you

wanted...maybe a frisbee...I am not so good with
frisbees, tho...used em' more for rollin' than throwin'
back in tha day, if you knowaddimean?...haha"...

"really? you are amusing to yourself, at the very
least, I suppose...anyway, I gotta go...I can smell
something
on the wind...um, off in the distance, I mean...where
humans can't, soooo....yeah, keep your chin up
and all...don't whistle for me, I'll howl for you and
all that"..."arf,arf...arf......arf.........arf"............

"SPARKY!?!?! Sparky!? dammit, come
back...ohh...I hate these moments...friends passing
on and not sure
what to say to anybody anymore...wait...is that? he's
coming back...good ole sparky...come here, boy!"

"woof, woooof" *pant pant pant* "i said "wooof"...
pant pant pant

"you sound different, sparky...that run really got the
better of you...you gonna be ok?"

"i could use some water...it is hot in here...um,
around here"...

"sure, here you go...hey, if you want, I could be
your temporary master for awhile, I wouldn't
mind"...

"master? are you kiddin' me? I know how to operate
an oxygen tank...I am nobody's chump...uh...I
mean...look...
I might have meant to say something else...I
mean"...

"hey, you are not sparky...that is a dog suit...and not
a good one at that...god, my eyes are getting
bad...come here
a second and let me...don't fight me...ow, shit...how
did you get a dog suit with claws so sharp?
dammit...hold still...holy sheep dip!!! MICHELLE
BACHMANN? what the hell are you doing here?'

"(sniffle sniffle) You have found me out, razor...I
have secretly been in love with scott wannberg
for so long now...I I I ...I just can't believe he is
gone...first Rick Perry and now this...I can't take it...
I wanted to reach out to scott so many times...no
one knows me like he does...I see myself in every
one
of his works of art in writing"...

"well, he did write about you often, is that what you
mean?"

"yes, he was critical on a personal level, but he just
really had me down...I mean...I don't even think
the little jewish carpenter in the sky knows me as
well as scott wannberg does...I wanna be his dog...
I wanna be his dog...I can't take it"...

"whoa, off the dickie's, mrs. bachmann...get
down...you are surly bitch, mam...DOWN NOW!!!"

"oh, I'm so sorry...my bladder is so tiny these
days...and texas is so big...not as big as scott's heart,
tho...
he made me wanna forget that stumpjumper from
taxas...forget the whole teabagged last one of those

corn fed constituents in Iowa...he made me wanna
be a L L"...(crumpled in sobs)

"an LL? what the hell is an LL?"

"oh, don't make me say it...a a a..a LIBERAL
LUTHERAN...oh god...oh god....please...I don't
wanna live...please...I wanna be scott's dog...I
wanna be sparky..."

"hey, where is sparky, anyway?"

...on a spiral trail to a worldy place where there are
no dogs or masters, just eternal conversations
that go round and round where every character actor
and actress that ever trickled into the kodachrome
and technicolor borealis is remembered as far more
valuable than the leading man...this is where the
constituency of loving fairness dwells...that is
where sparky and scott are now...watching a
classic movie channel that never ends with tv
westerns in between every movie...always going
back and forth with wisdom and insight that is just a
lil' further off into the future...not so far that
you don't notice as long as you never forget that
there is where you need to be...right now, so get
there
  before ya'll come back now, ya hear?...

Minding My Own Isness

what am I if not this right now?
call me what you have to
call me what you have
call me by a name
call me out now
call me now
call me
call
me
now
I am
here
in this
moment
waiting for
the next moment
that is happening now
as
now is always the moment
I have been waiting for all along
call me from this moment into the next

Process #1

let in the fullness of it all
fear may block the necessary
so let go completely with all
the dizzying effects that
come with that
layer overwhelming joy over fear
over hope over anger over love
over grief over heat over pain
over cold over sex over piss
over hurt over lust over think
over blood over hunger over lost
over wander over all over lovers
over war over birth over murder
over sick over spasm over tears
over semen over feast over shit
over hugs over moans over laughter
again & again & again & again
until   until   until   until

work with the words in essence
work with the sound in assonance
work the tempo in time and edit
rewind edit rewind edit rewind
until the reels smoke from
spinning wildly in your mind

now focus hard on to it macro in thought
 now step back wide shot of the big picture

grab a hold of something that you hate
 to keep it close
let go of something you love & never get it back
push out demons & angels alike
invite whatever walks by in the darkness

to come into your light
let it examine you
as much as
you will
examine   it
 truncate & expand
with assured vision
that this is your truth in total
every word in line in break in pause
in running thought as it slows to dripping
into droplets of sounds of phonetics of language
acutely aware of itself as yours in truth & style as it
should be
pass it on like this if you can & be ready to take it
back at a moments notice
to run it through the raw breakdown of the mill in
your mind
once more
to work it into something more accurate
 for the next moment
to be more mathematically correct in its estimation
of your
unguarded soul as it sits in the center your body
somewhere between your mind & your heart
telling on your truth as if to snitch you
out to the last love you can find
along the terrible road to
creation

now get to work
make something else
before you get caught
waiting for praise that
never meant shit to
the source of your truth
in the first place

Process #2

bang into the fragile
smash all that is fake
break all that can be
broken
for the sake of it
bring her back
with honeyed words
chosen wisely
send her running
with vinegar venom
spit out in anger
lament her loss
in sadness so
deep it echoes
bring her back
with lust so hot
it burns like a flame
a raging fire
lit as a last resort
to keep from
freezing
to death

stand alone
for a moment
to acknowledge
what you have done
to take it all in
then wait for a sign
to move forward
into a new beginning

Process #3

sing in celebration
dance in celebration
love in celebration

fuck in lustful glory
fuck for all its worth
fuck like you might
get paid for it
if you are good
if you are a whore
it doesn't matter
you need to do it
the way a blade is
sharpened against
a stone
cooled &
lubricated
by the water
of eternal life

kill to be righteous
kill to be glorified
kill to eliminate
competition
kill to eliminate
the basest fears
of living
of dying
of being
discovered
as unworthy
in the face
of an enemies
relentless charge

spare money to make the world more thrifty
spare lives to make mercy your creed
spare attention to detail in order
to preserve a basic truth
about yourself
guard all this sparingly
as it will serve you in times of famine
when she no longer seems to care to guide you
when her hand is missing from your heart
when nothing can be conjured
on the coldest nights alone
or in the hottest drought
of a burning sun
drying up
blistering
scorching
the last
essence
of your evaporating life
as it becomes sand & dust
to be blown about by the breath
of a laughing muse who is now
& finally
done with you

Selling Panties

We parted ways a while ago, but,
thanks to modern technology,
we still keep in touch online
through the miracle of the internet.
I still love her wild beauty.
I still miss her need for when the world was
all loneliness for the both of us and we got
lost in ecstatic misery inside each other.
I miss it for about 10 seconds tops.
She is a sex machine cum loud.
A real rootin' tootin' pornstar.
She is a media frenzy of ejaculating spectacle,
lining her pockets with the currency of the sex
trade. I don't watch her scenes, but I smile when I
see a banner ad that advertizes some product she is
a part of.

Recent turmoil in the biz has her calling me this
morning.
"Hey, Raze, whatcha doin'?" she asks with a purr.
She has perfected a few things, I can tell because
my belly tightens all the way down.
"Thinkin' bout a few things, now I am thinkin' bout
you, mostly."
I say in my most aloof exhale of past desires lost to
time never again.
"I got a proposition for ya, I need you, Daddy, you
still love me?"
I almost laugh, it is so good to be needed though,
needed by her velocity against the heavens like we
would be stars together shooting across all the
cosmos into the milky way of the night

like supercharged supernovas arcing onto Venus'
neckline like dirty bedazzled space demons of lust
streaking into orbit, colliding in a cloud of glittering
wet splashes of ultraviolet lightning…
"What's yer bag, mama? Let me hear your twisted
little thoughts on this."
I lay back and listen to the black light spider
spin her sticky web.

Turns out she is not doing any scenes lately, but
has tested AIM perfect anyway. She has a lotta
guys that wanna give her bread for panties on
the web sight, hitting her up by email.
She wants to link herself to my writing and have me
write her into my erotica the way I used to do
(she says that made her so happy then).
She says she is gettin' hot just thinking about it,
"you getting hot too, Daddy?"
"I am following you, but I want to hear more about
the part where Daddy gets paid, baby."
She breaths a deep huff and moans a lil' bit like
pleasure, but I hear the contempt of a spoiled lil' girl
getting her candy taken away too soon,
"allllright, fucker."
She lays it out with a little less drama in her voice,
but still a lot of sex.
I suppose she can't help that,
I don't fault her none for it, either.
She lays it all out simple enough.
She wants me to come fuck her with no condoms.
She wants me to come do it and to not pull out.
She wants to make video clips of it that
she wants to send to the email trick with
the pair of panties that she puts on afterward.
A thousand dollars a pop, she says, I get 200,
50 more if I send them a poem with it.

A poem about how I love to fill her up with it
so it all drips down out of her into these here panties
that the trick would be holding in their hand while
reading the poem.
They can even read the poem while they play the
video as they take deep breaths off of the silky
encrusted panties.
She says it is like they get the full experience of our
art combined, our genetic material mixed in
together forever as dried inspiration for moments in
future fantasy of abandoned lust into the future
orgasm to come.
More than worth the G for admission.
She sells it so good I can smell her manipulation
behind every word. I listen to her elation as she
spells it out in a win-win-win situation for all.
I tell her I'll think about it seriously.
I tell her it is a brilliant marketing plan.
She giggles before she says "I love you".
I smile before I say "I love you, too, lil' mama."
I have never been paid that much to publish my
writing up until then.
I don't know any publishers who would make me an
offer that would come anywhere close to matching
the potential of this one.
I suppose the economy might make it possible soon.
If it's getting to the sex industry like this, then a
publisher might ask me to come inside them
any day now.

Sitting Down for a Moment as Gary Snyder walks Away

so early becomes so late becomes so early again
like a spiral staircase of dreams and trials
each one dissolves into the next
no angels with trumpets
to herald us forward
no vacant being
of existence
leaving us
for dead
or
alone
here now
the wisest is
the young daughter
of the craftpeople's church
where the family beckons all
to come back into the fold of the town
located on the outskirts of the great city
that is part of a like-minded country of folks
who have all built something here together as one
where they say
  in all places blessed I may still find loneliness
there is no despair in it for me as I know you will
   always be waiting
to welcome me back into something akin to
 a home in the dusk
lit by the last magic
beholding failing beams of translucent glory
overwhelming all these considerations of
philosopher's words: the last moment of breath
                              of heartquake
                            of shiver
                       of death____of peace

Happy Birthday to Tony Scibella

I was a kid in a dying america that heard
  the voices of the lady
I was lost in a tangled kipling jungle book
  of rhymey words like
a wild Mowgli taming jungle beasts as if
  I had forgotten my own humanity
only to fall against the sword of my ancestors
  just before
the pearly dawn like
the dying gladiators of the lost generation
who never wrote a letter to Rimbaud
never sent Gertrude a birthday card
never cried for Zelda in her asylum
never drank Cuba Libres til sunrise with Papa
never were aware of their own condition
but they left behind hunks of moldy rye bread
that dropped delicious crumbs
that moved the wheels of my infant stroller
until I could walk among words
  of my own assemblage

Dickinson seemed so terrified of future terrorists
that she named
with a cunning predictability
  from her solitude so well
that I always wished for her to
  list them all that I might know them from
  my hope for future solitudes
  that I secretly yearned for so nervously
as I shook hands with J.C. Oates in hopes
something would
rub off on me
I never knew what terrors were until

I stood before the world
with my own words formed into broken lines
 of redemptive pleas for forgiveness
I was born after the Venice beats time,
 growing older & older
during the Temple of Man time
as I built my personal temple of doom
 I read their words & wept alone
because I was more deeply involved
 in the territorial warfare
 that was blamed on gangs but won by realtors
 & new home buyers

I am friends with Tony's words as they comfort me
in my travel worn soul
that finds it harder to hug the Venice shoreline now
than in the past
when it seemed a perfect fit even down to the
decadent pier
of Pacific Ocean Park that stands gloriously intact
in black and white photos now
but was full color jaggedness for my youthful frame
as it glided and collided
between it's mortally wounded obstacles
hidden from under the late breaking waves
of the unpeaceful pacific ocean womb
with a rocky breaker placenta
that birthed dreams into
new reality   new vision   new voice
newest voice of an old muse that always
 brings me home
 like I have
only known homelessness & prison
while the world knew something else
I am learning slowly   catching up slowly
                    healing slowly

Pacific Ocean Park is long gone beneath
the jealous waves of modern conformity
My name of names no longer adorns the fallen
walls of
demolished shower facilities where I would lose &
regain & lose & regain
all my faculties in those rust aged facilities
over & over again
leaving gifts in abandoned
shopping carts owned by the real immortals
of no worldliness
known on this plane of reality
by talking fast to their
telephone totem pole messiahs
asking for shelter
from the words
that drop like truncheons on their
methadone fragile skulls
running in a primordial frenzy
like chastened goonie birds in full flight from reality
seagulls proclaiming them as kindred spirits as they
leave their mortal bodies behind like stamped out
cigarette butts clutching tattered clothing lined
with free newspapers
from beyond baroque's front stoop

Scibella, Long, Thomas, Perkoff, Rios, Metzler,
Margolis & Taylor all beat this path wide and large
as I stabbed & fumbled years later through
drunkeness punktuated by
opiated amphetemined
coca senselessness
that made moments feel better
as the big picture got worse
as I won a two way ticket to the big house
more times than should be allowed

as I am so grateful that it was
as the ghosts I left behind in
Chino, Vacaville, San Quentin, El Reno, St Cloud,
Lompoc, Santa Rita & Rikers
wonder what lottery screwed them over to give me
winning parole numbers that I could not lose alone

alone is how the numbers leave me
 on Tony's birthday
as it is honored by S.A.'s words that honor me in
unison as
Iris nurtures my manuscripts
 as Shira gives me shelter
as Bucky, Doug, Rafael, Al, Luis, Mike, Frank &
S.A. provide words I read
that give me support
when I was young I was told the only thing greater
than friends
are pallbearers
who love their burden
as if it were weightless

I have so many gifts I would never dispute the
existence of any god
that gives them to my atheist mind turned mad
as I walk along in the caffeinated rain
down echo park blvd to the bookstore that lies
somewhere between
the temple of man & the house of spirits
I walk with the ghost of ishi as he leads me forward
as he tells me what it was like to be the very last
one of all that were counted before
 at the end of the   longest line
Ishi becomes more mortal as I walk
Ishi takes my hand to lead me to the truth
Ishi says "I am only the last wild Indian in books,

in truth I lived inside your heart all this time
as long as you didn't deny me
because there will never be a last of anything"
together we share mashed acorn soup & skip stones
across the echo park reservoir
from the boathouse to the duck infested island
 as Ishi says
 "laurel and hardy are   immortal spirits
that move silent movie pianos up & down the stairs
like happy cherubs
instead of depression riddled Sisyphus symbols
tortured by the new Hollywood CGI God"
Ishi speaks words so good & pure they honor
all the best words
of a greatness in purity
ever spoken by anyone
(Ishi leaves but tells me to
 look for him
on Dia de los Muertos
 wandering down Olvera St.
 Ishi says he will be the one dressed
                    as a pre-Colombian skeleton)
I am in love with the ancient words of Ishi,
 but they are the most modern words I have
 ever heard or read
it gives relief to me
that I may not speak so well
I may not write so well
but if I can just pour it forth as pure as I can
then the sacrifices that you made for me
might have more meaning tonight

Happy Birthday, Tony
I might have met you in person
 had I not driven so fast all night
across great divides with criminal intent

& a trunk full of deliverance
I might have shook your hand if I had heeded
all the words that echoed off of the mountains
from Colorado to the jetty off of Venice Beach
during sunset
facing the last glow as it disappeared past
the purple majestic mountains of Santa Monica
I might have been your friend if you had lived
longer, who knows?
I might be your friend now
 if you would have my humble words
inside your tangible spirit of eternal poems
they are all that's left of my connection
to the dying gladiators of all the lost generations
before me now__after I am gone as well

Questions, Questions

the answer is never in the exclamation
no matter how much bravado rolls forth
from the gaping maws of victorious saints
the answer is seldom heard or recognized
whispered in hushed voices that beg pardons
afterward   they never meant to give it away
they rarely know they even have it on their lips
the answer walks away incognito always looking
both ways   it is frolicking in the bird bath when
no one is there to see its joy   it is crying in the
back
of the homeless shelter while the tv is up too loud
for
anyone to notice or hear   it is with you now in a
soft embrace   right at your side like an old
friend or
a newborn idea   ready to give rancor to doubt
enough to
instill hope into the last moments of dusky sunsets
before
all is darkness on every horizon imaginable
the answer is
in motion all about like fireflies near
a porch light   waiting
for one last story before we all turn in
    we all turn into it
it is the only answer to every question
ever asked   there it goes

Buddy Collette Gets His Rest

shining shoes on 95th & Compton
Mingus had the bigger shine box
swinging jazz for cents to barely make a dollar
that splits into trio into quartet into sextet
into all night jazz jam sessions
like when Bird got out of Camarillo
Buddy is there with
Dexter, Morgan, Red, Gay & Co.
Bird is healthy so he shuts it down
Like everyone hoped he would
there is a school in session
every night__all night
Buddy moves from
session to session
from sax to flute
to clarinet
& back to sax
from record to record
back to session
ahead to leader
from club to club
steady man, steady
man, was he steady
steady as the bottom
of the beat as
friends become legends
become ghosts
become memories
as he finally makes his exit at 89
to go be the bandleader
with all the saints as
 they go marching in
marching into cool west coast jazz
swing so low as they go

as they go, man, go
these cats act like they
  no longer know
all those lyrics that they
 blow & blow
go now, buddy, go
still playing on my radio
don't you ever go
anywhere
but here
right now
with that sound
that cat left us__gifted as
we are by it's everlasting tone
with that sound
it might get quiet
but it never has
to be silent
anywhere
anymore
anytime
go on, Buddy,
go, man
make that
sound
forever
in my mind
forever there
with that sound
get your rest now
with that sound
forever

Emperor Norton

called the world his oyster
opened it one day just
to eat it up raw, pearl & all
took the title for himself
wore the hat & uniform
even printed his own
cash
that the barkeeps
gladly accepted
to keep him entertaining
as he gave speeches
bequeathed titles
stood on street corners
like royalty was real
he showed the world
what a charade
any crown could be
all you had to do
was take a title
for your own
stand proud
stand as tall
as your legs
could hold you
the rest
was just ceremony
left for fools to follow

Cold August Morning in The Point

a cold morning wind blows across the point
 in August
as a woman smokes a cigarette lazy
 on a Sunday morning porch
looking at a lazier street that meanders up a hill
 right in front of her gaze
record temperatures are being deadly
 somewhere else
here, the birds sing quick and low, as if to not excite
a move
in any direction, up or down

there is no season here right now at this moment
this frozen little town that resembles a time
 when there was industry
hundred year old train tracks rust slow
 under random use
their great purpose barely discernible
 as a history lesson on a faded sign
half covered by seagull excrement
 blown to a dry bleached masking
 by the wind off the bay
this spot once helped save a nations honor
as it pumped an effort
outward to meet the terrible foe of liberty
 broadcast by a crippled
president who asked for mercy from god
as well as god's blessings
for government underneath these fog banked shores
of mass production
that time has left this place so far in the past today

it is vaguely noticeable that war was once an effort
once a sacrifice

as the weather has seemed to have left this place
like the jobs of long ago
there is a museum down the road
 to Rosie
 the Riveter, an advertising legend
a colorful promotion of innocence, sexuality &
industry all rolled into one
people noticed her likeness as much as Uncle Sam
& the bald eagle
you would have thought it would have been a
national goal
to never have unemployment again

all these ideals faded away from the wrecks of
shipyards and brickyards
to the dissolving of the economy here long ago
long before credit swaps & dot com & housing
bubbles burst out loud

the point had been passed by way before all that
 in favor of cheap labor markets
in other countries more torn by war & poverty
 in the last fifty years
the desperation that runs through
Richmond, California
has never been enough
to inspire presidential candor
 or congressional calls to action in all that time
it grew like an invisible virus & infested all the
rusting hulks of leftover industry
moving all the way north, east & south that it could
leaving behind memories of all night shipyards,
auto production, construction, manufacturing
that are like a wall street hangover today, making it
easier to trade on the pepto-dismal

numbers game that became the inherent holy grail
of the market economy
that had lost the physicality of an actual
marketplace,
  where people traded in goods & services
in its lonesome wake of destruction so long ago

this small town that sits in the fog of doom and the
vapors of the last industry, petrochemical
languishes for the laughter of the dancehalls nightly
filled under bright moons over Point Molate
as it desires once again to put all the railroad cars
 in motion
              to deliver more than just a random
scattering of Japanese cars that are barely
 less   radioactive
 than the turnips of Chernobyl
each ghost that wanders the town square at night
 knew what it was like
for a brief moment to hear the sound of industry
 humming so loud
              so proud
 that it seemed like the world
 would never want for anything, anymore
with real liberty & real justice for all
at least for those who had faith in politics
 a faith
that has now become the wisp of smoke
tailing away from the end of a cigarette
held by a woman who looks across a quiet street
at an uncertain future full of uncertain hope
buffered by a lost faith in anything
ever said politically, ever again
to anyone who can see
what has been lost   what has never been found

On A Walk With Poets At The Huntington

walking along pathways into verbiage jungles
 of english gardens
coming out into clearing of genkan entry way
 into nipponese
tea gardens that sing with buddhist bells
 of birdsongs
accompanied with a slight timpani rhythm
 of babbling brook
rushing down rocks under dense foliage
 fanning above with dragonfly witness to footsteps
passing along intricate pathways up to the threshold
of tarmac crossings into a tea garden
 of a chinese tradition
that unfolds with hand hewn hunan cobblestones
that capture all footfalls
guiding them into ponds
 of peaceful contemplation
 on stone bridges arcing
above the clamoring carp
 of multi-colored luminescence
hidden in brackish waters as they playfully gasp
 for entrance into conversation
 as each one contains
a mythological poet who trades words for
moonlight dignity
when all visitors have tread homeward
 to leave them
reciting their own litanies inspired
 by the conversations
of mortal wonderment that transpires
 on the granite bridges that shadow the shallows
 of their liquid quagmire
of this crowded solitude among turtles
 that languish for sunlight

in their amphibious shells of natural rewards
everywhere there is safety in this pond
a peacefulness as birds fly overhead
these carp seize nothing more
than morsels that are known
as words that are common
as carp in the ocean
but never more
beautiful as
they are
right here
right now

It Comes On About Now In The Dark Silence

looking for something
among all of this
searching for something
amidst all of you
finding something that
doesn't make sense
confusion
frustration
complication

delineating a path toward
an eternal mystery
reckoning through the darkest hour
to make it into the quiet moment
of a peace that only happens right now
until the anticipation
of the oncoming
unknown
misunderstanding
is upon
the moment of peace
ending it right there
in that moment

who what when why where?

internal clocks and compass
cease to function properly
internal voices are mumbling
about something indiscernible

what to do now?

there is

there is no one
there is no one
to love
there is no one
to love
me

right now
right
now

On Writing

I take my beatings for not fitting into molds
for not following instructions
for doing my thing
for doing the wrong thing
then I start writing
I lose out on opportunity and love
lose cash and prizes
gain something back
lose it all again
get another chance
they keep coming
one after one
sometimes
two by two
or even
three by three
but, I keep writing
I take flight into the world of no certain destination
moving like a target that is hard to hit
near misses and head on collisions
almost take me out for good
almost only counts in horseshoes and hand grenades
so I keep writing
I get cut open and live with scar tissue
get shot and it is through and through
my spleen survives it all
my liver falls for hep
fire water burns my heart
I get run down by wheels but get up later
the breaks heal slow and crooked, but they heal
I watch others not be so lucky
I keep writing
I watch others get born and buried

funerals in fields and ashes spread on oceans
I feel my friends blood seep out quickly
leaving me behind with open eyes of shock
I wake up next to a lover who dies in the night
I find another in a hot tub of her own blood soup
I watch another die the slow cancer dance
I hear MS stop a beautiful heart
I sit alone in silence for days
I keep writing
I make many friends for life in my travels
the dope takes so many
the violence and the prisons take so many more
drunken driving into nothingness like
darwinian angels of mercy takes
my little girl away while I
languish in a cold room
on a steel cot
puking my forgiveness
into steel toilets for two
I keep writing
I hear warning shots from invisible guard towers
in my restless sleep forever
watch indoctrination into death
for believers of an honor that was
betrayed long ago by human greed
I keep writing
I ride trains across midnight prairies
hoping to become dust devils above corn fields
as I look at the Brooklyn Bridge become
the Golden Gate become an old stone transom
across the Mississippi River that I walk across
alone after love is just a dead cat that I give
a viking funeral to with lighter fluid on a guitar case
barge
in the dark cold river below
and I have to keep writing

I have to move my fingers
across the page even when
they are bloody and broken
or cramping into claws of
eternal damnation that tells
me not to quit or give up or
give in I just have to keep
writing
even as I sit here writing this
on a laptop in echo park
not knowing what will
happen next
listening to birds
dogs in the distance
helicopters in the air
I am moved to keep my fingers moving
to keep writing still
in case I missed something
that might be catching up to me

Legacy of the Best

punked out by
all the betrayals
inside the mind

all the 10 dollar word poetry
all the big bravado boasts
all the superior positions
all the farts of dinosaurs
still circling the earth
keeping the water level
just low enough
for now

beat down by the motion
beat upon by the movement
the rush to judgment
the common thievery
among the honorable
the uncommon honor
among the thieves

"me thinks thou dost protest too much"

some say you might know
this devil
maybe even
more than you should
some say you should
avoid the devil
you don't
know
altogether

ask any ghost

of any buried
culture
haunting
our DNA today

devil's don't seem to differ
much at all
once it is
too late
to revive
what has been
torn asunder
and inevitably
someday
the dinosaur fart
will have the last laugh___at last

truthful love poems

on a nature walk
along the border
between the
refinery &
the ghetto
where the weeds
burst w/
flowers & fruit

pain in the belly
is fuel for a poet
as love moves
too fast
farther
up ahead

love is younger
love is lighter
in its step
than the poet

skip away
   skip away
this pain
is the poem
love leaving
behind
poetry
for life

the greatest
poem
was never
written

because
the poet
was in love
with only
love
filling
the heart

the vacuum
of love moving
away
writes
in the
mind
immediately
        skip away
   skip away
        skip away
until there
is a poem
written
from
loss
of
blood
from
an emptiness
in the heart

an ode to the children
on the beach
throwing
stones
    skipping them
        away
          one after another

wondering
what
poems
mean to
old people
chasing each other
under the sun filled sky
upon the weed filled paths
between the refinery
& the ghetto
so far from the fun
of the polluted beach
where they skip stones
in wonderment
without knowing
the sadness
of skipping
as it moves
love
further away
        so much
              further away

Quickie

rubbing the fleshy lightning rod
inside the meat curtains
of velvet thunder
until the skies burst open & placate
 the drought lands
with a down pour
pushing out temperatures like the tropics
of every known zodiac sign alive
listing the names that are called in tongues
speaking a crescendo of god
o god o god o godly goddessness o o o ooo
all gods be named in this parade of words be
damned until kingdom cum
        make it rain   make it rain   make it rain
licking stormy petals of flowers
blushing with multicolored perspiration
pollinating everything the drenching touch of it
covers with stickiness
laminating it all shiny
with the underpinnings of wrought pleasure
sending ravens soaring above macaws
cackling at parrots promenading
it all floats down like the fluff of daffodils
 turned slimy and spittle
layers itself against the conscious need
 for a rag or a shirt or something
maybe boxers or even panties, just to wipe up the
mess
  so you can lay back
                        catch your breath
                        count   your blessing
      sink into it all
        before the moment
                    passes   you by

Palindromic Dream Cycle

awake   awakening
slowing down   deescalating
drifting off   disintegrating
envisioning something   pixelating
subconscious   surreality
rapid eye movement   destabilized thoughts
twisting journey   conjured imagery
conjured imagery   twisting journey
destabilized thoughts   rapid eye movement
surreality   subconscious
pixelating   envisioning something
disintegrating   drifting off
deescalating   slowing down
awakening   awake

Lady Ga Ga Calls Me
On Dali's Lobster Telephone

candy graphics coated her skin
like a daytona hot rod dripping
down the road where no more
clocks melted the time away
from elongated elegance of
digitally remastered circus animals
while a guilty looking guy ritchie
spanks his fag holding hand
against his throbbing sensation
as he squints his eyes for a
madonna adorned memory
below a floating crucifix
from a latent pepsi commercial
turned into a coca-cola product
placement against the cries of
young girls forced to hide
broomsticks from correctional
lenses that obscure the visceral
demons of a tarantino dreamscape
in full blown cinemascope mouthwash
for the light of the words that cum to
mind when the thoughts find hands
slipping into the space between bellies
and elastic beyonce looking plastic
in KY conditioner and filter tipped
relaxer that auto jacks you on the road
as it under projects the eject button
to over define your avatar as it fucks
applications for iPhones with Microsoft
macro hard zoom look into the future
of the fourth dimension reich's furor

take a breath savory lick
spit in your hand wax nostalgic
wipe it back and forth
up and down
back and forth
deeper into this

it was stroboscopic in the frontal
lobes of the cortex rather than the
backdoor of the suggestive medulla
oblongatta that used to ooze forth
slow primordial essence under your
ear near the nape of your neck like
black molasses in an iron range
blizzard blowing in high speed
slow motion that is now replaced
by flash drive test pattern warnings
for nuclear hologram webbing that
catches more than just andalusian
eyeballs in razor fast editing devices
that promote a polysexual frenzy in
an amorphous box of multi-colored
condoms that taste like magic glow
worms circling shiny tongues covered
in female ejaculate that polishes the
new world prison floors and happily
gives a fisted vagina cigarette advertising
approval so that there cannot be any
mistake about the ambiguity of the action
just the jump cut repetition that makes
preachers go blind with ambition
blond with an act of contrition
in burning tan beds of ignition
hairless faces see bodies abolished
as nair wears short shorts spraying
out in sprinkled anecdotes of gasm

covering all faces who watch too
closely with a creamy emission
that is a synthetic emulsification
of what has taken the place of
adolescent masturbation without
a good narcotic left in sight so
the officer can apprehend the
last offender and finish what
is left of the last greasy noir
burger now that no cows are
left to reproduce more of
themselves in 8-track ecstasy
because they have all gone
bull dagger with
strapped on mooldos
riding solar powered
sybian lawnmowers
turned mound
polishers til it
all sparkles
bright

look at it
in its own
resolution
it's horrible
but like thumbnail porno
in my loneliness
on a cold night
there is something
there for me
when she just
isn't

Walk Onto The Quiet Mesa Alone
for Jim Carroll

the tenor of the moment creates the vision
looking out to sea with the caps of waves
cresting out past the potato patch reef
wondering what drake saw here that
both horrified and intrigued him so
gold in the lagoon was only light
glimmering off the tidal pools
or the heads of playful seals
water was everywhere in
streams full of salmon
running back and forth
in their greedy spawn
but the trees, o the trees
majestic and tall   all pushing above
towering into the horizon edge like
sawtooth contrasts on every ridge
standing watch for the infinite epoch
that unfolds in the beckoning bay below
the salt wisdom springs forth eternal
until the gunshot breaks the silence
that is never heard until the body has
begun a dance with rot and decay
that dangles tendon like busted
banjo strings
curls back the lips into a grimace
all the same
leaves sonnet and haiku alike
indiscernible from babbling brooks
running down a crevasse underneath
the sentinel of oak and redwood
the burden of understanding left
in a natural setting
for an unnatural rhythm

sync has been lost
sinking down
all those meanings
to all those things
lost
like a fortune in a teacup
while the egrets stand still in the marsh
the pelicans dive into the churning aqua ribbons
that undulate at the sandy edges of hazy memories
where the fog bank is lurking like a blanket
accusation
this won't end right here
this won't end right   here

News That Hurts To Talk About

the woman I love
 is ok so far
she will bleed it out
 blood leaves
 hope
 fully
 her
life stays
hope
 fully
love stays
 still,
for now
there is gratitude
for what is left
 even for
what is lost
this is what
can't be run from
 anymore
hope
fully
something is left
 maybe even
stronger
 after
the blood
 is done
 running out
somewhat
& for the most part
for what is left, for what stays behind
hope
fully

The Falcon In Flight
for Robert Duncan

a shrouded falcon waits to fly
 with a disciplined anticipation
every muscle & tendon taught as suspension wires
that hold the golden gate aloft above the entrance
 to the bay

the falcon sees no perspective
 from its cloaked darkness
it plays out turns in the sky as it closes on the prey
to seek the acceptance of a master it loves
trained for this in daily regimen
given praising rewards for its prowess
it gathers strength from each motion
it holds its head up, alert and waiting
for ultimate perspective to be revealed
birds of the sky flee in fear of its talons
sharpened black pointed differences
admonished for overzealous maneuvers
against the master's arm that holds it high
tethered to a master's hold on the falconer's rest
a beautiful bird of prey waiting to behold
 its own magnificence
turning circles & dives & aerial twists
 in its minds keen eye
free falling in dives as it moves__ glides__ soars
after its mark
the sparrow__ the lark__ the pigeon__ the canary__
the crow__ the starling__
all know that the falcon's shadow is a fearful sight
on any day of flight
these more common birds may even have
 unsettled dreams of a falcon's menace
 when they are shivering chicks

    sleeping in nests, newly hatched
dreams that turn to nightmares as they are
set upon by the fatal talons in their last moment
before jarring awake
stirring into the reality that the falcon
that is trained to satiate
for the reward of pride & nourishment
 is the most deadly ending
to the simple traces of a birds life
lived in a worm & seed fed neutrality

the falcon soars above all the admonishments
 of the common birds against it, even
as the falcon relishes any opportunity
 to prove itself in any manner
dressed in hood & tether
 it stretches its gilded shiny wings
as the hood is removed it preens
 in a new selfless love
  before it sets out
  in a rapid flight
for a new attack
with the heart beating in the chest
 so fast__ so heavy
this is the chance
that it has been hatched
from desire for
 so long ago
this steadfast falcon that has always
 wanted to please
  an eternal mother
that has always wanted to protect this land
from skies to low valleys
that has always sought to end the admonishment
 of master and siblings
wanting to rightfully fly its mission

on sharpened turns of valiant wings
it flies forth out of darkness into a light that it has
never known until now
a light it has only seen in dreams of days
 that were always hoped for
above green fields
spiraling through the skies searching for the
freedom to serve its holy master, love

Picking Up Buffalo Nickels Outside The Dakota

they call us american myths
but mythos needs religion
as much as religion needs
mythos
the feed line gets broken
hunting and killing it's way
back to starvation
we didn't invent glass
but we shattered it
to make political counterpoints
more dramatic
pleasure that was so elusive
is now the main commodity
of a collapsing market
that cannot reassure
it's own existence
regimes look better
in advertisements that use
reality show characters
to sell diplomatic envoy ideas
on secret digital rolodex
cold war encoding devices
that never saw the bullet coming
only presidents falling
into strawberry fields
forever
where they have erected new stores
in many convenient locations
here to help you
with rock bottom prices
to give you a varied diversity of monotheistic
choices
that keep some of us hostage
while most of us fight over them

until the birthday is less and less sacred
if it even really ever was
to begin with
in the first place
you will be able to talk about it
amongst yourselves
after the funeral services
that is how plans work
for the living
for the dying
the living always win
every argument
except the last one
characters get assassinated
more quickly than people
so most will die here
with a dead character
falling before them
as anger is the passion
that most feel easiest about
you only have to be right about it
once
to be right about it forever

The Eternal Dance Of Catullus and Lesbia

her light and energy burst into the world
it creates a dark chasm when it is
extinguished all of
a sudden

he would eclipse her
twice in every lifetime

she would always die too young
the first time he found her

he would always be too old
the second time she came
back into his life

he always feared that she would never search for
him
she never knew the name Catullus
in her memory again
just the words
of his poems

he could hear her music and see her art everywhere
he felt her inside his breast always and forever
he would never fully accept his fate
he would never fully concede
his doom to love, unrequited

jealous gods have their way
his words brought
tears
to their eyes

envy
to their hearts

doomed to play an eternal tragedy
in intervals throughout time
these two lovers would
pass each other in
life's dawn and dusk
twice in every
lifetime
half of his life's work
of heartfelt poems
would be concrete
proclamations of
beauty in love
beauty in life
no matter how much
form is misunderstood
by other eyes upon his art

the other half would be painful laments
twisted lines expressing the internal tortures
of love torn from within without any mercy
words that cut into emptiness like flames
cutting wounds into the darkest of tombs

time and time again they would be resurrected by
the gods
only to be out of sync in vain attempts to right the
eternal clock

her music and art searching for his poems and
words
the bloodletting of centuries begins again with
every rebirth
the madness increases with every near miss

mercy would be to end the cycle
except for the fact that
the cycle is the source
of love in the human condition
all gods and lovers are powerless
to alter its course
once it is set in motion
lovers will search for each other
in the foreboding metaphor
of ships passing in the night
on still, dark waters
without glimpsing the
others sails or mast
or the contrast of moonrise
after sunset or
sunrise as the moon
still hangs for a moment
never touching the sun
in a million years
lest calamity
take us all
then love
would be
left alone
forever

The Difference Between Free and Freedom

to walk on the playground
as a naive child looking for love
you had to take an ass whooping
just to get playtime started

firecrackers from tijuana were as illegal
as all the housekeepers, dishwashers and fruit
pickers
that lived in the trailer park shanty of the desert
wash
but, sales by the brick could earn money
for a summer shackled by poverty

the example was set in stone somewhere
it seemed that infallible and permanent
play sports to get out of here
join the marine corps to get out if that failed
risk your life and imprisonment if those choices
failed
huff glue, get tattooed, fight for the hood til you die
if you just have no ambition to leave here

if you left on your own you would most surely
spend moments alone in quiet places that exist
between bedlam and chaos, horror and sacrifice
listening to the story of your genetics told there
in silent whispers of doubted facts and fairy tales
the codes so overlapped and mixed up
there would be no clear allegiance
ever pledged to anything more
than simple survival
dug out of dark
concrete corners

run for your life now and again
as long as life will have you
run to the ocean sides
to the redwood forests
across the fruited plains
over purple mountains
standing truly majestic
over runaway vistas

hope might live over every horizon
might be pursued in every direction

evade detection by armed and dangerous
authorities waving flags on the sleeves
every moment until you are burned alive
by your own vigilance inside spoons
inside small pipes of your own ingenious
makings

avoid extinction by living on the inside
far more than it showed on the outside

roll it up, ball it up, give it up
over and over and over again
to the trauma and the pain
the turmoil and the chains
your back breaks under the weight
of the work you were never promised
in this promised land that was promised
to someone else and their children and
their grand children and so on until
you realize that the reservations are too real
to ever go away and the history books just say
whatever
so smugly in the face of petrified tears
that you realize the mother of all

realizations

this land is like the playground
where you were first forced to fight
against your will
when all you wanted was to play
for a moment
but, that moment never came
and if it did
you missed it
so now you miss the point
of the celebration as well

there are people that are
missing things
there are people that have
found things
there are people that are
wanting things

I have been all three
but,
this was never freedom
for me

Morning Cup O' Joe

forming a hectic morning into fragments
that might stick together
a piecework artistry of chaotic whirls
akin to tumbled dice
the building blocks of mortal promise undone
this stitch in time is rendering all
this liquid brew of oily bean
ground into a steaming submission
that is it's normal state
except it may
save our lives in its
radiant ripples of warming effect
as it awakens what was once left to die
so that there may be another chance at salvation
or at least a hope that we can ring the alarm together
before the migratory obligation is returned
to the surging gene pool
that washes away the last effective breath that is
gasped for
 in convulsion
this cup of coffee is no longer as normal as it first
may have seemed, now that
the last drop is good for a another new awakening
on another new day of promise
yet to be fulfilled
                    as per the usual
                    abnormalcy
                    of this life
                    in this world

stop

I was
raised up
like this

I neva
hate a hustle,
I jus' hate
bein' hustl'd

do what you
gotta do
but,
don't be
surprised
when I
feel the need
to stop you

WCW

it is easy to hear her words
in the phone conversation
it can't be taken for granted
it must be a passed down___a blessing
                                          of sorts

so my son puts my grand daughter
on the phone now

these simple gifts
these precious moments
like paintings of wax fruit
            or
little girls with big eyes
            or
velvet elvis crying in the ghetto

where is my heart in all of that?
dusty books pointed a way long ago
the direction was to go against the current
swim it or swallow it
never stop

looking for the mentor of my minds eye
searching out the feelings that are left
like crumbs on a lonely trail of tears

you said for us to make the honey into homespun
threads of love that tied every line together
brought every word into sunlight
gave every rhyme a shelter in
a torrent of digital rain

it is cleaner in my mind thanks to

your broom
of phrases
simpler times call for simpler words
            so we can
        come
down
        from all mountain tops to sit by your fire
old man with candies in his pocket
 hands
them out one by one

even if another bitter one
gets unwrapped
 in my hand
tears of joy fill my eyes for what I
                        taste & smell
tagged with your words as lines
unbroken   until broken

            then reformed
            as brittle
                    pieces
                        gathered in

your   wheelbarrow
            of ripened fruit
                preserved forever

                        fresh
                as love
                in any season

The Wind & The Bridge

seems something is always
falling
hurtling back towards the earth
breaking all the records for the fall
that happened the last time
we were raised
pushing back against it
hoping for some new help
we lose some every time
another fall occurs   it would seem hopeless
it would seem futile
if no one ever tried to make it   again
all the way across as the wind blows
losing all the balances ever gained
there would be no shame in it
a slight chorus drifts out on the breeze
"never give up, never give up, never give up"
the attempts move us forward
as much as they move us across
the divide is never so much conquered
as it is a means to many ends
what else would we do, in the mean time?
stay on separate sides of a longing chasm
losing all that is helpful as we languish
together in doubt
biding time until someone tries to rally us
bringing in the newest ones to help
so another bridge can be built
while the wind only knows

how to blow
& blow
& blow

Incoming Storm Patterns

lured in by it all
the spectacle
the sounds
like the
sirens
of old
myths
come
and
gone
a
child
left
alone
mother-
less
cries
out
the
thunder
of explosions
this is no longer
anyone's party or
even a show of force

this is where the rhetoric stops
this is where the body count increases
this is the moment that control came out of hiding
no longer patient with the way the crowd had
gathered
one too many times

Tow Truck For Two In The Tule Fog At Night

the discipline of thought ...   prescribed...
forgotten
along the two lane blacktop heading north
fears
     ambiguous ideas... broken shells of ghosts...
this mist is thick as car accidents
 ladders across lanes
dreams of wrecked vehicles...
 arranged like decorations
     skidmarks into wild hearts...
   taken by beauty
     in vulnerable moments
       rolling   rolling   rolling   on purpose
snatched away like broken hulks of
                         unworkable fears
     small burns of light through the haze
stop...
       the wind of boxes at high speed...   moving on
desires beliefs faith *all holding fast like chains...*
just as you see the end.... it comes back to the...
never like before... *always like a   ghost...*
apparitions
       illusions of confused optics...choose to be
blinded...
     drive away with all the burdens into the night...
not like thieves.... not like pharoahs... *no longer
like ghosts*
the fog clears as if it favors a better outcome, as if it
gives *purpose...*
groggy bewildered... never really lost... *finding
momentum...*
         lost time from broken clocks ... fix and
clean *themselves*

it is a cab over a road in the distance...   it is help for
fallen travel... *the traveling traveler*
        pulled apart machinery...
hearts on mend... last chance *for...*
peacefulness   along the unseen roads into
blur...
            ...going too fast...   for these conditions...

My Perfect Cock

no crowing before dawn submits the loving
 beads of light
unless the cock crows for no one but itself

born with a curse that should have meant
 an advantage
endowed with the certain ability of a flightless bird
shown to be extravagant in flowered daydreams
 of lustful bloom

just meted out justice will do
 in times of battle
with sword & blade

plaintive souls rest easy now
 that the villain
gets its due

the paramours of taste
would spit this out
at our combined feet
for the impracticality
of swerved lines__ swollen with contusion

sinewy rascal of veined hologram
 made into surreal packaging material

like a pillow, many have knelt to it,
eased a cheek upon it
taken comfort from its presence
 deep inside
the folds of truth

some have wept at its absence,

written poem & ode to its loss

some have damned themselves
 for taking on such a harbinger of joy
knowing joyful moments run fleetingly
 away from us all at times
capturing them like wanton butterflies
 gone stark raving mad
lost in interwoven nets of conquering doom
drowning in silky jism desires

there is no rhyme or reason to behold
 in its cuckolded form
it has only been a messenger of my love,
even in the most addled moments
even when it was just a ruse to overrun
 the embattlements of desire

just to hold, just to be held, just to feel
 until the feeling hurts so well

just to be a part of you, connected to something,
if only for a moment, if only one moment more
than this will ever permit again

Data Echo Chamber DaDa

you are alive born
you are born alive
you
you
you
you are
you are
you are
you are go
you are go
you are go
you are going
you are going
you are going
you are going to
you are going to
you are going to
you are going to die
you are going to die
you are going to die
you are dying
you are dying
you are dying
you are dead
you are dead
you are dead
you are never dead
you are undead
you are re
you are re-started
you are re-programmed
you are in syndication
you are archived
you have been surveyed

you are beneficial data
you are reborn
you are alive born
you are born alive

Perish The Quicksilver Thought

blessed virgin
was the real name of the shepherd who saw the star
so sacred and bright shining unto the unwilling flesh
raw and rubbed with salt from ancient seas
extravagant butcher of bleeding hearts
laying waste to all the unforgiven
sins of tumult and desire
now lost in barren wild
shifting into love
become real
for us all
here and
now

Scott's last words to me…

errant comet seeks retribution-
will only smash into agreed upon
        section of earth-
      conductor absentia
      is hard on one's sense
      of abdominal self-worth
so this is what S.A.'s poetry bomb looks like?...that
rascal

bedlam and chaos were disbarred last month for
shady shenanigans

(i shall work on this exercise anon. a nun?)

wrap me up and smoke me slow. retired? baby,
you're just starting out. the engines are
 at full throttle and the sky nods its assent when you
let its rain cool you.
 the last arrowhead just eclipsed its shaft and the
dancing city is born every time you ask it
 to rise up from its ashes. go doc go
i'm in the front pew, reverend doc and you are
waltzing me through the barbed wire of our time
 with your large large super heart. score a big one
for the giddy gipper. those big prisons are midgets
 when you walk up to them and sing.
a patriot's raga. i will send you the lyrics of steve
goodman's the ballad of penny evans.
 a giant forest of america's need to remember its
backbeat. rock me forth on your world tour of
   damn yes
 this what we are capable of...
it soirees. gracias

very clear sailing. the water is resonant

139

you ride the high country squared. in fact, you're a
damn poet. ring the bells. tell everyone to listen up.
 razor is singing...paul robeson hears you
truly moving, lyrical. the marin county jail could
and can never hold your spirit. we never mean to
get mad. we just do. robert earl keen sums it up
best....the road goes on forever but the party never
ends. thanks, friend
rolling along the ongoing process with a river in my
hand and the life inside the tone as it glows with
some enduring empathy...wail, wail, wail

el camino real by tennessee razor....my favorite
play....yes, indeed....now if s.a. writes a 59 caddy
riff...strong soiree, amigo...

fucking a as they say....strother martin was a big
whitman fan...i did i him for my master's orals at sf
state...i did him? that sounds like a federal
offense...walt whitman's america by reynolds
rocks...yeah yeah yeah...mr.bard

had a hearing, had a heart
you just must agree
razor sings
whewwwwwwwwwwwwwwwwwww. .to reiterate
dr.prof griffin....yep

heady and heavy and noirish and goofy and all
encompassing mountain climbing of the spirit in
dark high gear...almost a novel in its history and
impressionistic implication...you're robert mitchum
in the bates motel and the ghosts are biting....now
will i be able to relax???? great driving music here,
mr razor
enriching meditation and the distant lights of
monterey are steinbecking you as we speak

and here i am reading a book about a man wrongly
sentenced for murder in oklahoma...
actually made a vow to get back to reading and
watching movies instead of being sucked
 into this thing...as usual you are accessibly
empathetic and clear sailing in your riffs...
 keep em coming...strong, thoughtful and human...
riding the highest country of all, amigo...your heart
is a large continent and you do rhythm it well
 with your ability to sing down the language that
contains us...as sparky says...beautiful...ride on

Bottle Notes from a Drunken Holidazed Oasis (S.O.S.)

drowning in shotglass
suicide note turned to ash
burnt up inside bottle, send help...
the only thing
on the horizon is
a flotation device
made up of
forgetfulness

The Road To Hell Is Lined With Billboards

it is already judgment day in japan
but nobody is all that concerned
keep sticking kelp up your ass
hoping for a faith cure from it
hunkered down for the winter
when it is just in time for spring

flooding gets diverted to you
never really washing away sin
barely drowning any sorrow
hardly raising up the ocean
in an ice age of global warmth

plagues have already been
working on us all overtime
antibacterial soap has leeched
into the gene pool like the rare
vinegar of evil piss on the tin roof
of the coastal golf course villages

if you let the earth bleed out
into blacks pools of terra blood
covering every porous indention
with a slick lubricated doom
it would become the last news show
before anyone really gave a shit
on the too late times

nothing ever happens tomorrow
without some type of conspiracy
born in the bowels of yesterday
makes you wonder how it all got
started in the first place because
the last place you looked was where

it was hiding all along except for the
part you thought was more clever
than anyone had ever seen before

that is actually the part where you
live everyday like it was judgment
live everyday like it was the last
live everyday for the same reason
that
you are willing to die a little more
for
day in and day out
you don't need a sign to tell you that and if you do,
what would the point of that be?

Song of the Plum Jar Preserve
for Robert Creeley

These are the sure footed sounds
of horses riding on long ago lands.

I wonder at my life inside of the sugar
filled worlds of amberly lighted delights.

She made this glass sterile before
she made this mixture boil with love.

I can taste the dankness of lost artscapes
surrounding me as I spin into the radiant

waves of molten looking wires inside the
working toaster. These biscuits must be
warm to melt the butter, spread the jam.

35,000 years until now. Where is the blood
that has been replaced with dreams of

melt, of sweetness? Brought to life again
as shadows across our tongues that twist.

That twist together in this eternal spiral
of a knot that won't ever be undone.

Or ever done again. Melting like this. Ever.

w4m

"I'm looking for a guy who can
fulfill my needs.
I love giving head.
I also love going clubbing with my friends."
Fallen Goddess, w4m, 32

she is searching for me
missing the part
where I decide one thing
confusing it with a part
where I decide another

"I'm looking for a man who can
fulfill my sexual needs.
I love anal.
I also love going clubbing with my friends."
Tired of jerks!! heh - w4m

I am searching for her
almost finding a clue
to her deleted past
I continue on
into the last
darkness

"I am a real woman who is looking for
a gentleman in a situation that is ongoing and
discreet
in which we can both benefit.
Perhaps you are not looking for a serious
relationship
or have other responsibilities?
I am low key
and can keep

your secret.
You should be educated, generous, and kind.
In the age range of 30 to 45.
I am STD free and clean and expect that of you.
I am 32 years old, educated, very curvy, sexy, and
busty.
Dark hair, brown eyes, and olive skin.
Please tell me a little bit about yourself and I look
forward to hearing from you!
PLEASE RESPOND ONLY IF YOU ARE
SERIOUS AND MEET THIS CRITERIA."
S........E........X........Y........L....I....C.....O.....U....S -
w4m

I want to respond
in all seriousness
but I suffer from
criteria confusion
I am lower than keys
been busted by busty
not ready for entanglements
enmeshments or strategies
that might dissuade me from
my fear and suffering
too much perfection
makes for flaccid learning
curves that define a
procreative bent
I am better off
anonymously
attacking the
lying mouths
of midnight
glory holes
before I
settle for

her truth
here

"So....just like the title says....I've never had an
orgasm during sex!
I need a man to show me how it feels! I am 23..
long brown hair, brown eyes, 125lbs, 5'6
very cute with a lil bubble butt ;)...
if you know how to work it
if you know to make me cum
you need to email me now"
need my first orgasm - w4m - 23

where are the men? where are the men?
they are needed desperately
they have been neglect in
the teachings of man
passed down like
holy scriptures
replaced by
blackened eyes
for unrequited beers
like bills gone unpaid
until there is no more chance
of bankruptcy or bail out
just repossessed hearts drug
away in the back seat of squad cars
or in the coroner's van
telling no more tales of woe
searching no more for fantastical
results of an engine that never ran
on fuel but was fueled by errant desires

I hope she finds her happiness tonight
if only for a moment
I hope it doesn't cost her physical rent

on her body and soul
laying there like it was meant to be
abandoned by the superhighway
in visquine bags of regret

maybe there is a place where
there is a hope that is
more brave than mine
sitting on a stool
slapping faith on the ass
in a dingy bar while it laughs
out loud

puffing on a cigar
hope blows smoke
into the face of faith
as faith coughs
hope says
with much confidence
"relax, let me buy you another round
I meet everyone this way."

Waiting, Pt. 1 (in Oakland Intrn'l while reading Tony Scibella's *The Kid In America*)

 waiting for a flight in Oakland airport, looking out
on baywater as it flows around runways & future
prospects of flight trying to get to L A today to read
a few words off the page in Venice in the place
Beyond in the place Baroque in the canal town the
carnale town the lil' place in my heart the big ace
 up my sleeve where I learned the difference
between dead & killed & killer where art meant no
job blues
 but blue art painted bigger pictures for me like an
ocean that is never quite blue, mo' green like the
money that gets chased around & around I nvr cld
stop it, did not like be in poor so scratch & sniff &
shoot my way thru to a freeway offramp nearer to u
so I could find the glue that might keep the world
2gether long
enough to be a sep rate truth thatno one could steal
away in the night w/ gov't permission like
paperwork that meant doom that chased me into
sleepless thoughts so far away from it all…from
rooms &hopes &pens &words into torn muscled
terror of bikini fatefulness always w/ passion
&more passion like last night but sometimes a long
time in between like legs & promises & a brochure
that sold something so long ago I forgot who I was
writing to bcuz they died so many dead so many
dying the last sacred death unknown to me so many
already buried already burntup already ashes
scattered poems all that is left standing cept fer kids
& kids make the world go round so I did this fer the
kids, (once they mistakenly call'd me a kid too, so
take it like a grownup, you lil' punks) don't tell em
nothing tho, let em figure it out, they all got that

light inside like I did burning out all the way to
brightness in the darkest moments we did not come
to bury ceasar we all came on the salad tossed up
greener than the waves off Venice on a winter day
of stormy tides & santa ana winds blowing chapped
lipped dirty blond girls from Midwest retreats onto
casual boardwalk strolls under seagulls that shat out
last nights foraged poems onto the heads of
incendiary tourists turning beet red burned out
cheek boned masters of destiny reaping the
whirlwinds of falling markets all around a world
mall that might as well go back to the stone age for
all I care as long as you solar power battery charge
the vibrators that the muse uses to get her clit just
right & give the goods all night & we smile together
as we hear the sounds of music everwhere
(evreewear)…everywhere…everywhere a dance is
underway a foot is about to tap & move & maybe
even spin in a way it has never spun before…if you
go go go fast enuff you might make it…you just
might make it tonight…if you go now…what the
hell you waitn' for, kid? get the hell outta here
quick…before the Spanish mausoleum sountrack
gets you in its everlovin' grasp like the ball'd up
fists of angry angels wit' dirty aces, all blackn'd out
like bums on bitch's, ex-ex'sfor eyes like bipolar
bears turn'd to cannibals before the summer melt
cums early to the polar heart that never mattered
until it raised your ocean level and called you, it
wants to see what you got…nobody's bluffing in
choir's poker with cheap suit's unenjoyment check
cashing boutique pride pumping out of every house
speaker tht sez the same thing twice (remember,
these are the same folks what tried to sell you a
death ray to kill commie missles, but now those
missles are coming froma different place and

deathrays don't sell like they used to)…not when there are perfectly good returnees returning on their knees to knit a conundrum of perplexities that never meant shit to a Sodom and Gomorrah historian like yourself as the rabid atheists spit in the god eye of doom and dare death to cross the line fantastic…death winces at the unmiracle of it all and waxes back to when vinyl was where hits were kept and brink's were trucks full of money, not the place we left the world accidentally on purpose, and tony, o tony can't you come back to the five and dime dope spot where the broken dealer an' hustled prankster gave the last dime that ever made a phone call before poems became cellular fertilizer that killed the next crop before the muse could be reawakened cuz she just rolled over and said "I heard enuff bitchin' to last an eternity, which is all the time I have left"…I quit my complainin' a while ago as the plane begins to board like a big bus ride into the sky and I am hoping that the security technician groped me on purpose, at least…just need one last injustice to keep it all blind…there is not a hand I been dealt I haven't had to bluff on…even when I pocket flush the royal canard right out the old whoosecow…

Waiting, Pt. 2

...it is the prominent moment that counts in the
record book, but all those other moments had
families, too...they felt things, did things, some
ordinary, some strange, some defy all
explanation...no one wants to have t explain this
stuff that happens, they want it to be self
explanatory, they want it t sell, sell, sell...sold...gone
on too far on a cool breeze blown at a cold time
when the latent prints were left behind in the form
of icicle daggers through the heart, nothing left for
the crime channel or the court tv or the kardashian
shopping network or even the cooking channels to
stew up into some blend of cathartic bonanza happy
cowboy ending on the rootin' tootin' ponderosa
where the lil' doggies are not afraid of the hoss that
walks backwards toward them...I told the maitre'
dee at the airport deli to make me a reuben w/
corned beef n mustard n he told me he did not like
poetry which I dug to mean he didn't like peoms w/
the poets in them, which I dug wild (the whole "I"
always being about me is a drag to read, everypoet
being an "I" already, its 2 much sometimes, don't u
agree?), cuz I don't want to be here I would rather
be there watching the hitch up happen in the
common man's happenstance, altho the cold is still
more common than anything (could you close that
window, please) and don't, under any
circumstances, type BOMB in this moment as the
taxi down the runaway has been postponed because
of a pre-existing condition so as to not jeopardize
all the clever things that they can do with social
security now that there is an election going on they
can erase the last remnants of slavery, but don't tell
those guys over there cuz they don't seem like they

would understand and that might make things worse for the rest of them, knowaddimean? nudge/nudge wink/wink....this is where the astertrix would stop you and give you some supplemental information bout how low we can go in this dick chopping, bushwhacking contest that has become the digression of the times while wild billionaires run around with the idea that there is plenty more where that came from, whatever that was, & don't worry too much because you are gonna bring the ratings down & we might lose the asian subtitles that are necessary to keep investment potential up as well as trade agreements agreeable...why shouldn't a third of the planet own everything, just so there would be a new sheriff that knew the score...the time machine has been running overtime as the wheels of fortune turn & twist in the wind of no articular determination, so as to proliferate a new, more virile form of communication that involves human centrifuges that could produce new clear wintertime landscapes that could mean christ mast all year round for the kids (they'll love that, is the word on the street) no more happy new year's will be needed so put away all the noisemakers & quit rocking the boat so much cuz we are all in this liferaft together n it ain't gonna get easier until you all learn to go easy into the night as the blades are now readyto slice n dice all the needy peeples into neat lil' ribbons that will be tied into bows on the everyday present under the neverending tree of lifetime subscriptions to a more posterior standing in the community of what is passing for cultural stimulation these days...they are ready now, for boreding...

Tub
for Naima

he writes the lonely letters
alone in the next room

she takes the drunken bath
alone in the other room

there is just a wall between them
a hallway that connects them
each just inside their own
doorway

the music plays so loud
but, they can still hear
each other
breathing

the sound breaks the glass-heart'd demons
shatters them into shards & pieces
screaming for hopeless chaos
inside their heads

he will grab her up in his arms
later on when he is finished
spent onto the page
unable to squeeze
more of it out

he takes a pause to turn down the sound
she steps out of the steamy tub

he can hear the water gurgle
as it rolls down the drain
as he tries to finish

like death is racing
him to the end
of it all

it is a race you know
& every once in a
great while
he can catch a glimpse
of the nemesis
in the mirror

but, he knows from experience
looking over your shoulder
is the best way to lose
a close race at the end
even though
winning
was never his strong point

the thought now would be
maybe meet her in hallway
while there is still moisture
lingering on the skin
lingering in the air
no words, it only adds
unnecessary tension
there is enough winding
of the spring by now

wood creaks as steps draw nearer
to each other at an intersection
that approaches in the next moment
bodies become crossroads
marked freshly cleaned &
dirty minded
paved with all the intention

that hearts can muster
that blood can swell
that juice can flow
in an angry world
on a mistrustful night
flesh against flesh at last
forgetting any hopes
forgetting the meaning
of anything that can't be
washed away in the water later

Walking Up Blue Mountain
for Gregory Isaacs

a hot night walking along steep roads that become
goat rails
a rack on my back as we hum tunes to keep going
ankles itching from the bites of sand fleas
there is no glamour in this business
except that we are more free
here in the jungle
than in the city
what we smuggle
is really of such little concern
to all the forces of the universe
as the bright moon rises above blue mountain
as the envelope of stars guides us to our destiny
we are proud ganja runners who work hard to make
it
we are the music of life to the shanty town dreamers
in the city
I hum a tune of lovers rock for a girl I lost touch
with on a beach
in California that I may never see again because
loneliness is like that
I hum along with the tune as the tune hums along
with me in unison to
heartbeats in my head that play the metronome of
my soul as it makes
the pace steady as the feet move me forward like a
westbound train
kicking dust into billows as if my feet were
steaming along
the ganja farmers will welcome us and fill our racks
for the long journey back down the mountain
maybe I will see the girl that tends the fire

in their shanty camp at night
she always looks at me
with eyes that smile
as bright as the stars
up in the sky tonight
tomorrow will find me
alone again on the beach
my work done with some
money in my pocket
looking out to sea
waiting for a ship
that might be a sign
that might never come
until it is time to go back
up the mountain again
on another ganja run

Correspondence With Baudrillard Afterlife

riding wildly as a bike messenger with no brakes
through the late night streets of Reims
letters that should never be read
lest they induce an insanity
from a fervent
belief system

we talk of broken bottles nesting upon the
blue shells
of brown breasted robin's eggs in double bested
nesting habitats of minimal lighting cues that
signal for Brechtian manuscripts with no
curtains to call home or scenery to call
attention away from the life yet to be
yielded from the jagged edged cuts
in the paper trail of lost Chekovian
firestorms that come every hundred
years through the black forests of
beastial progress as you warn the
world that only madmen would buy
a rusty plow from the wealth of Engels
that came with instructions written in
an Hegellistic tantric prose in order to
dispel all the rumors of rampant Marxism
in the tea party arguments as they prepare
to deconstruct the only art worth making as
Bataille screams out to Barthes on his suicidal
website "say something now, Roland, the world
is still not listening to your fetishistic podcasts on
spiritual dilemmas that used to sound like English
punk rock songs but never American gangster rap
because that was more like Jean warning us all that
houses of cards fall because we all see a beauty in
the way cards fly across town on the chilly winds as

winter approaches and leaves dry out and become
just more jetsam and flotsam for the turbines of
literary mediocrity that parades and lampoons
 into the worrisome minds of
those that have drained themselves
 into the long looks of
a broken mirror with no light being directed
 at the grotesque
details of all the beautiful flaws that would
 reject themselves
as insignificant only to the writer
 that writes and writes but
never collaborates until the day they put flame
 to paper
in their only hope to send you
 the letter they told you they
would have sent had the mail been a priority above
all the broken bottles that cover the blue
 shell fragments
where the still born robins are fed
 meaningless worms
that will soon be feeding on them
 in their last known nest

Jumbo's Clown Room #1

she danced with her
cocaine eyes becoming orbs
set free by the music

Loisaida Blues #112

the surge of sea water
washing over loisaida
will leave every ghost
intact, maybe even
add a few more
down in the tunnels
where the mole people
can't swim so well

the storms are always gentle
to the haunted remains
of the tenement museum
that preserves the memory
of the real horror show
modernism left in its tracks
such an awful century ago

when the wind blows just so
it still sounds like the walls
are crying for a mother
who will never come home again
or a father who should have stayed away
neither one matters to the current landlords
the rent is always paid in different shares
down the alphabetic avenues these days
gone, barely forgotten, but ghosts, all the same

the last falafel
come to this land from far a away land
a land of poets that spin mystical lines
into the forefront of the conscious groove
the sand in embrace with the moon up above
the dance of the earth against the sky as love
lies on the surface below the thin layer of air
in between what is substantial & what is
most surreal

hafez worked hard to remember
not what was written
but felt in the heart,
not so much the lines
as the beats
of the breaths
that came after the sounds
of words that were uttered

these are the most modest words
of a simple poet, heartfelt

there are bibles about how to write a poem
in the English language today
the correct forms to use as a construct
that might please
the educated palate
as it wanders the barren landscape
of poetry left undone
& great lines left unkempt

not enough buried lead in the gullies and canyons
to keep the sugar filled cliches from flooding the
common plains of wordsmithed meanings to
lives lost in the work of the muse and the scribe

sadly, the cafe was shut down today,
good neighbors they were
the coffee was brewed with love
 over the sound of music
with a background of conversation
 that seemed to guide
the most elaborate dance
 of neighborhood life, thriving

I ordered the last falafel
 she would make, with a tear
 in my eye
the rumor is that a subway fast food chain
 will take over soon
10 years after she fled her Persia
 she watches everything she built
with her husband, Muhamid, together,
come crumbling down
on the last day of the quaint café
 where I was always addressed
as neighbor, friend...these are things
 that can't be regained
so easily, these are the things
 that stick in our guts & our hearts
as we go back & forth
 to work everyday, wondering
 when the hammer
 will come down
on our fragile dreams...
in the mean time, I savor every last bite
of the last falafel she will make
in the humble Cafe Altura
as it closes down under clouds
so swollen with gray, they are
 about to cry for us all

Spoiled

"tomato or no tomato?"
I dunno, whatta ya think?

"tomato, cooked or raw?"
I dunno, cooked? or is that more work for you?

"I like to slice them thin, then broil them and put
them on top of the fritatta."
You must love me or something.

"Its love. Do you think mint is good on pineapple?"
Like mint leaves?
"Ya, like a garnish or a seasoning."
Never had it like that.
"And drink this glass of aloe vera juice now."
It tastes like dish soap.
"It is good for you, I want you to live a little
longer."
Careful for what you want for, mama

*(the smell of cooking coming from the kitchen is
intoxicating)*

"Here you go, senor razor, do you want hot sauce?"
Simon, should I eat the fresh fruit first?

"It's better for your digestion."

I would rather have tapatio than tabasco if you have
it

"Sure, but you already used the Tabasco."

I will use both, thank you

"Are you going to stay on the computer?"
I am working out an idea, this is good, very good,
 I will eat while I type.

"Did you try it without any hot sauce?"
No, but I can taste the goodness through the hot
sauce, I love it.

"Do you like the macha tea? I frothed the almond
milk separately."
It is delicious, are you just going to watch me eat?

"That is what I like to do best."
It feels like you are waiting for me to finish or
something.

"I want you to choke me with your cock some more
when you are finished."

(maybe, I think to myself, just maybe)

*her eyes glisten and sparkle with intent as she stabs
me with her lustful stare*
It seems like a fair trade to me this morning, I will
think about it as I eat this.

"Just sneak up on me and do it, daddy, whenever
your ready."

Whose gonna do the dishes?

"I'll take care of everything, don't you worry."

Sounds good to me.

Jumbo's Clown Room #2

inverted over money
we are all tension against poles
flesh defies gravity

Dennis Hopper

It was way back in the 80's. I had been working for
Toni Basil on several music videos, running
playback, helping with rehearsal choreography, 1st
AD on set and even learning post supervision. I also
worked as a PA occasionally, or background or
worked on music with different people. Always
hoping for a break that might get me off the grind of
the streets of LA. I was out in the clubs or at shows
at night, occasionally running my own after hours
clubs and selling whatever contraband I could to
whoever wanted it to keep my life moving and
trying to stay out of the way of the cops. I spent all
my down time in Venice, surfing and sleeping to get
my strength back to attack the world again and
again.

    Then, one day, I was invited to a dinner party
at Dennis Hopper's pad thrown by his daughter. I
showed early because I had brought a few party
favors that I didn't want anyone to get the jump on
me in the sales department over if I showed up late
and the knock was already served. That's how it was
in those days, people would ask for something and
if you got there in time you made the sale, if
somebody showed up before you, well with certain
products that people have a hard time waiting for
especially, you would have to sell it to someone else
and that might mean roaming around to find a
person in need, which is how people got caught
transporting.

    I was already an abscondee from parole,
and wanted by the police for questioning in some
unsavory situations involving people that they had
heard I was in contact with. I needed to watch my
fucking back while I did everything. It was an 80's

double life and many people crashed and burned back then running similar hustles. I brought   a few things with me and headed out earlier than I usually would, a bit nervous, a bit anxious.

Plus, it was Dennis Hopper's pad, so I am sure I used that as motivation to be early rather than prompt, even. I didn't often get invited to such places. It paid off nicely, too.

He was there, I was introduced by one of his daughter's friends, we struck up a conversation that he seemed interested in maintaining with me. I chatted with him about working with Toni Basil and Karen Black, who he had worked with in an acid and booze fueled shoot on location in New Orleans. We talked of that, of Apocalypse Now, Walter Murch, insanity, John Ford, graffiti art, James Dean and Sal Mineo, photography, my personal knowledge of prison and gangs, social justice, his new movie that was almost done, the odds of me ever making it in the biz, my recent experience running a second unit shoot for Cannon Pictures' Angel III, and how they had sent more film and other scripts and actors at me for 6 days straight and I shot so much extra footage, inadvertently, for several other Golan/Globus projects with little sleep and not much pay. Crew members kept switching out while I furiously made schedules by hand and called the day while deciding on the next shot list. I told him the upside for me was that I was moving speed and coke to the crew and above the line, which made up for the lack of a proper rate, and I felt the experience had really proven I was ready to direct something.

He agreed with me when I expressed how I felt there was lot of bullshit people in Hollywood and they were just in the way. He told me about being in the western bad guy pool with guys like Bruce Dern and the struggle to get in where he could direct and finally produce on his own terms, and how drugs and booze and insanity had cost him ground many times. I remember I almost blew it by mentioning that his place will look killer when it is finished, because the walls were not all there and bare wires were everywhere and he gave me a puzzled look and said, simply, "It is finished." Which I just laughed off, realizing what a fucking faux paux I had made.

I remember he put his hand on my shoulder and said, "I have a feeling you are the next Orson Welles in the making. You just can't let them discourage you. Keep fighting for your vision."

People started showing up and he excused himself to go work on finishing touches for his new film, *Colors*. He left us and I never saw him again where we spoke so candidly. I felt pretty damn good and I was out on the town all night and a few days later I told some people to fuck off because I felt I was pretty validated by the experience. Dennis Fucking Hopper had proclaimed my genius, compared me to one of the greats, and I was selling blow to one of Altman's guys who was blowing smoke at me about backing for a thing I had written. I usually was pretty bullshit proof, but the idea of being the next Orson Welles and my immediate experience misled me pretty well. I never made that script, it was "lost" and years later a suspiciously similar film was made at a boutique studio with some familiar folks

171

involved. I was on the run again by then, watching the film in a theater somewhere in the mid-west or back east. Thinking about Dennis Hopper and Orson Welles and Robert Altman and Walter Murch and John Ford and Robert Evans, coke deals gone bad in after hours clubs and my feelings regarding being a half Sicilian, part Apache in a world where neither mattered unless you were a character in a movie.

I was not gonna make a film anytime soon, that was apparent. But, I still held out hope, even til today, that I might make it back into film making someday. I have tried very earnestly the last few years, in a seemingly futile way. Fighting, fucking up, fighting some more. Over and over again. I might never make it out of that conundrum. I don't know how much Hopper was just bullshitting with me, he knew what I was and how I really made my money, it was not a well kept secret or anything, but, over the years, I have reflected on that 15 minute conversation many times and felt like the thing that stood out and can't be taken from me ever, is that Dennis Hopper really told me to keep fighting no matter what, to not give up. Whether he sincerely meant it or not, I will always be grateful for that.

Lost In The Formula: Rumi is in dreams as Naima is in reality?

tumbling out of cloud-like embrace of linen heavens
spilling onto hardwood floors like lost collections
 of dust
as the sound of nearby waves crush color wheels
 of sonic wisdom
into circular visions of love holding love
("this is all about love" said the broken heart
mending)
hiking into the wilderness barefoot
over rocks & thorns
the bewildered lover never touches the ground
 with feet
love walks on love walks on love like one foot
after another foot on a softening footpath
　　　love　　　　love　　　　　love　　　　love
　　　　　　love　　　　love　　　　love
looking into each others hearts to see a light
 is shining there
looking into a drop of water to see the ocean
 as whole you are both a part of
waves of bewilderment breaking overhead
amazed at all the amazing amazement
cloaks of bright lights are discarded
falling like cloudy waterfalls away
 as eyes send arrows into each other
sifting out all the bullshit thoughts of
trust this trust that what is meant by you? by yours?
you standing there to give to receive to want to hold
cascade away the sickness into the melting
 of sacred candles
set out in the windows of souls
 to guide the way home
guide the way to love

guide the way to lonely
 guide the way back
all are welcome to come into this light
  to build this light
soul by soul each one like a separate cell   each one
a piece of it all like a honeycomb of soul   of love
of serendipity in mindfulness   in love
as heads roll over heels heal over heartbreaks
new shoes blues requires you wear no more shoes
barefoot is the price of admission in this wilderness
searching for the life of it in wild grasses
 lining marshy estuary
running into lagoon full of heron and egret lurking
into tadpole pools
looking for no more rules of thought as the feet
 go off
of the path into brush
finding pumpkin spider hugs & dragonfly kisses
 abounding all around
lizards rolling under logs into burrows
 away from predator
 not to be prey
kissing starfish   kissing urchin
running past the first set of dunes whipped high
covered with scrubs & weeds & seagull seeds
spitting sandy licks
at coughing lost tongues turned into tonsils
too deep for feeling free

she turns away, only to come back
 when she wants to play with
a playful playfulness that trumps serious
 in the early morning
 every time

all this aging is changed to childhood in a kiss

with a laugh and a smile
we walk this garden like moonbeams
floating above moss
cool to the hotness of our skin
 burning into black milky-ness
losing all colors to contrast like cinematic pasts
uncovered
turning into the mist of vaporized mercury aloft
 in the lost
nakedness of unguarded moonlit trails
back into your heart

this is still about love as it is about to be lost
 on a lake of iron and ice
the winter takes on form as love begs
 to get one last chance
to transcend the transcendence
 into the beginning again
the chill of the wind is the world's heartless answer
but, love can lose all limbs & form to become
light as the wind with no sense of weather
this is what love wants when it is true
this is love when it is most honest

running headlong into the autumnal ocean like this
all beauty is all beauty is what is most beautiful
all about you right now
like robes of light hugging you
pushing the hair out of your face
the wind is playful with both of us
the heart is silent against the waves
as they crash and crash aloud
reciting the fate of all love
along this shoreline
unprotected
yet, saved for now nonetheless

War Prayer

look over this field
stiffen this resolve
let the resistance
never know a
moment
perishing

cover up the blind atoms
give anything away to
misshapen blast
patterns of eyes
closed too tight

deliver us the day with the night
conjure us a new world adventure
cleave away the fear that flags
have no home in nursery rhymes
speak softly of this affliction
as it spreads among the pools
that never dry away from the fields

let the children sleep until the first burst of anger
lights up the burial grounds of sadness overcome
by the happiness of the final moment of orphanage

at last, at last, at last
the revelry is never a sound
it is a vibration felt so low
that bending down never makes
room for any chance of clearance

everything will be measured
retold in stories
recounted in sorties

recalculated by patrol
reactivated by memory
memorialized by battle
you can't lose the fight
if the fight is never
finished with you

pray at last
for a finish,   then
before
it is too late
unless
it has become
too late
already
then
you can
just pray
for a forgiveness
that is most likely
another casualty
laying lifeless
in another field
that has yet to be
looked over

Breakout Thoughts Of Horses Dying On Race Tracks From Broken Legs

the voice inside always said bad man
now people say you are a nice guy

the area occupied was always controlled
now you only go where you are invited
grateful if you are able to show up

the world always seemed to be on the verge of
collapse
under the weight of its own injustice and weakness
now it is all you can do to try and be honest and just
in all your affairs and to support yourself by your
own hands

the darkness was a friend, a companion, a place to
catch your breath
the light was too bright, too much vulnerability to
be captured or exposed
now the darkness is full of fear and boundaries that
navigate you away
back into the light, over and over, until your eyes
don't feel safe there
anymore as your eyes adjust to the light more
quickly you try to be seen
so as to be present for life in the obvious brilliance
of the truth as it happens

you grieve your lost friend for a moment, from time
to time
nowhere to run, no place to hide, life in the open for
all eyes to see
they see you as you have never felt and you seem

new by their reckoning
but, inside you still hear bad man and know that
nice guy can't live alone
in the dark or stay still in the light as motion is
necessary to movement that
is required to get from the darkest depths to the
lightest heights and you look
for the valleys now to get some rest from the sway
and bend of the prism that is
your prison and your freedom that you now know
without separation of thought because
there is no guarantee that you were right about one
thing and it made you wrong about
everything else...catch a breath...stumble, but don't
fall...regain some balance and lean
forward into the force of life that carries you
forward for another step, a second step or
momentary loss of stasis that would have frozen
your dreams into darkness of what
was once under your control, your hold, your
influence...was it under you when you
thought you were under it or vice versa ??? vice
versed in experience that few really
have known so well, born into it like you were, a
secret covered by a lie that never
had a chance, that never gambled on anything
without calculated thought or at
least a second thought that was different from the
first and who knows what really
had gone down when the lights went out and it
became dark again and again and it
never occurred to anyone that maybe it was the dark
part of the nature of a nice guy
that would make a bad man come to light and few
have looked into those eyes
when the darkness overcame them and now there is

always a light on to find a way
out of the cataclysmic catacombs of catatonic
moments where there can be no
resolution from the brilliant to the dull and back to
the thud and the thump and
the last sound of the last sighting before it is
surrendered before the struggle
that nothing can win, but I know how to lose...a
thousand ways to lose...a million
ways to lose...you better smile when you call me a
loser today...you should really make it seem like
you wanted it to be funny...I might not get the
joke...

Upon Discovering cummings in My Bathroom
early in The Morning

what beacons lick light across window panes in
warning
 of perdition?
what, man, what? tell me of the grave, of the cost
and the award
 of it
silence the skeptics that crawl into oblivion's
shadows before your
spectral might, voice like heavenly trumpet to recall
an answer for
a primitive so advanced as myself, prostrate here
before
 your visage

what cur tells of the waste of souls formerly
drenched in brine now
left to dry upon the deserted docks of the
unemployed ferryman?
how many coins does a passage into this sacred fear
take such an
apparition as yourself, sir, such an automaton of
poetics
 in lower case?
those of us who have been chaste in your word
know it well
 as we sleep,
but you have come forth all moribund in gaiety and
frolic
 of lost spirit

expectation at this point would be tremor from such
a fierce

voice of spectorage
only this culled presence has no tongue with which
to answer, question or challenge
the eyes tell stories, though, of pain & abundance,
of song & withdrawal, life&death
all paradox in categorical admission of experience
in both feet cumming down into
both worlds, as esoteric as it all can now bend
 the light of countenance & betrayal
into one, a whole of submission & character that has
become
 a machine gun

this soul knows the machine gun, invented as if
it were just for typing about
bullets all molten hot & piercing bosom & brow
 only to cause decedents glory
in the realm of the manufactured psalm sung
by minstrels gathered in dark chambers
of lyric sensitivity against the rancor of personal
satisfaction
of a pleasure that even the mind's eye cannot see, so
there is a lacking
that matches the vision of a tongueless devil who
minced phrase
more than holy men mince words
for meat pies called bibles, o byblos, o lover

these smoky mirrors all about leave knaves words
 beheld by scoffing children
no sarcasm as to interdiction of faith
or a lack thereof, but knowledge of what
is born mechanical into futures of disgust & delight
 both shaded by a missing
fury of intellect that has been misplaced,
 for now, by groveling realities that

have been lost in a myriad of selfish poetics,
inspired thus, to trickle around us
pouring off of flaccid tongues, much like this
apparition, dribbling their cummings
like shredded prophylactics protruding from
dantiesque mouth holes
 in a formidable hell
of wordless preaching, just daft tongues of a
reasonless doubt
 in almighty bombs
as the new cure of modern madness that sent
 too many suits to the cleaners with
no receipt to redeem the proper garment
 from the counterperson who strove to
accommodate such a sorrow, such a laughable
sorrow, as a book burning bright
come too late for an electric world of vastly
 more shallow imaginations than have
ever preceded it with unpronounced acclaim at titles
of nothingness without hope
of a rebirth in worthy balance of an adversarial
 contradiction of souls piled high
on burning pyres of condemnation for lives less
lived
 than what was considered
acceptable to a limited imagination of a relentless
audience
 of masses that were
never a requirement to achieving anything
worthwhile
 in the history of creation

On Race, Gender and Crime
(in a misguided literary canon)

talking about a new book
with rodriguez who is not rodriguez
I am lopas who is not lopas
named by conquerors
my blood mixed up
with raped cells
that are told to
be more compliant
I have been named after
my favorite weapon of
cold blooded revenge
ever since I was 13

I need a theme for the book
Luis tells me honestly as
he rolls out his experience
with publishing many books
because of his love for the word
I am trying to publish again
it has been a very long time
I think back to the first poem
that ever got me in the mind
it was Poe's *el dorado* when
I was 5 years old it
rhymed me into the eyes
of the mad conquistador or
the insane english marauder
in a land unknown to them
looking for gold to steal
looking for virgins to sacrifice
on diseased cocks for christ
families to sacrifice on
steel swords & lances

families who were
running scared from
the invader's
well placed
cannon shot
now the
literary canon
still lays oppressive fire
down on me as I try to
share my story in a conquered tongue
being part white is being the part
that shows white but actions
speak loudest and white is
really only the tone of
the cleanest sheet that
is bleached of color
it is not a race of
men unless they are
firing upon your village
killing unarmed
women & children
in the place they had called "home"
since the last forever began

just to escape this dream
of my own genocide
my mind chases game in the hills
above the roswell plane where
ufo's pay for parking on the
sacred land of spirits as I
drink deep from the
devil's inkwell while
bats from the caverns fill
the sky at dusk
even the bugs here
have names that

depict their royal
standing in the
community

I snap back to
the image of my
son's handcuffed wrist
in a phoenix patrol car
just two weeks ago
his skin so much
darker than mine
I am proudly afraid
of what this world
is doing to him

Luis and I tell Hannah
how no one can know
you are writing poetry
in your cell
in prison
I speak in abstract tones
about the first man
I killed
in prison before they sent me
to Vacaville in chains to get shots
of lithium while Manson yelled for
cigarettes on the tier up above me

Hannah just wants my recipe for spread
she does not concern herself
with my history of violence
so I am relieved of guilt
for the moment
she used to drive
an ambulance so she
knows how heavy dead

bodies can get when you
have to carry them, but I had
to tell her we don't take them too
high up on a mountain to hide them
it is always
better in a low ditch of desert sand that
will accommodate many bags of lye to turn
it all into mystery again except for maybe a
few chicklet sized teeth that are no longer
pearls of wisdom as they hold no more
memory than that of butchered swine

I harken back to my first poets
Poe, Stevenson, Whitman, Kipling
when rhymes were standardized
not feared by academic pomp
or limerick tricked out by pop culture
sex industry hop pop music icons
fed to children like electric confetti
bukowski told me not to edit for the
black mountain manifesto that would
workshop away my soul and give
me a false beatnik identity
I read the last notes of brautigan
he accidently chose death
by his own hand
without even knowing it
rather than edits from untrusted friends
behind city lights at night gatherings
who raged as loud lions of soft
core wordsmithing that claimed outlaw
status after all the outlaws had been
hung or died from betrayal & syphillis
I flash to the memory of my first successful
head shot that caused a fatality
every time I hear the word outlaw

it was in my errant teenage years
I meant it to be a warning to buy
some time on a sunday night gone bad
in a parking lot of a park in mi varrio verdugo
the .22 splitting a skull at such a distance
was a horrifying miracle I can never undo
with prayer or offerings to the virgin
or the saints who are merely indigenous
spiritual movements hidden inside catholic relics

how many men does an outlaw have to kill before
he is an outlaw?
I read the women's words because of this question
that
has no answer I can perceive truthfully
ya all are bullshittin', dude, but its cool
down time is secondary to status
I remove cocks from the equation
heard enough about male superiority
in prison as I came and went
through the sally port
never the billy port

I read the words of acker,
mcnally, coleman, maybe,
cervenka, landry, lyfshin,
coppola,di prima, berry,
gehman, addonizio, tea,
bogen, calder, o-matic,
meyer, kirk, greathouse,
konesky, drehmer, beaudelle,
bruce, perl, moore, townsend, brager,
lowell, srygley-moore, bratten, tremiti,
clinton, wehr, krome, love, lunch, holiday,
blowdryer, lipuma, tamblyn, plath, auchterlonie,

bermejo, browne, mangiaracina, smolker,
candalaria...

a book in one hand, my hard cock in another
hopefully mine, but mostly I read alone
words echoing in vaginal chambers ring truer to my
ears than the old cock & ball stories that sounded
better on a prison yard & less appealing
in a county jail
always falling limp in a coffee shop with a list of
guys
waiting to hear themselves read their latest diatribe
about cool perspectives on their marginal life
because they are brave enough to be alcoholic
addict nerds cum performers a la rocky horror show
slam gesticulations with a perspective about a
similar
celebrated canon of men that you just wouldn't
relate to because that is how they got the grant
that paid for a prius or a fixed gear bike or
a bus pass (depending on grant size) & a
a poetry MFA & now they dodge the man
with no intention of paying back
their student loans...
living the outlaw life
...living outside the law that I am trying
to live inside of now in order to save my life...
I don't want to have to kill again
although I almost did kill this morning
(its just part of the job sometimes)
I practiced some restraint which might mean
benny blanco is coming back for me soon so
I could use a grant & some time to study
for my own MFA if I could get some space
to breathe again with the lifetime crushing
into my windpipe as I am forced to recite

my name with a throat full of pepper spray
& tear gas while people try to tell me
that I should be more cordial & that
I should fuck off for thinking I am at
the center of anything because they
really are & I just want to be in
the center of something but the
only thing I was ever allowed to
join was a prison gang & any
outlaw movement that laughs
behind my back about that
died without boots a long
time ago in a shootout
with a tomahawk
missile

fuck, I am just no good at this whole theme thing...

religious film criticism

gilgamesh never wanted much more
than to be everything to everyone
to be the center of it all at once
stones scratch steel, but steel
always cuts its way across
the distant blood horizon
of a nearby future
that sounds like
a far away
war
where the
three-legged race
towards the apocalypse
is always fixed for certain
a three way tie for the finish
a nobody wins, everybody loses
because one god had to be right about
something more than once in the history
of the godforsaken fearfulness of the masses
who all had a little bit more of old gilgamesh in
their ancient hearts than they had wisdom in their
futile attempts to conceive of a modern mind
 that could
think of a better way to go about making
a civilization on this loose rock
as it free floats through space toward its next
immanent disaster in the cosmos

exhaustion of it all

there is no arm around the world tonight
shooting stars fall away into the dark
all alone & cold

there is not much to be said about what hurts
there is a quiet hope that it will all heal soon
that plays against the strings of knowledge
the knowing that healing never ends
just like the hurting never stops

the wind blows sand across the deserted beach
pushing it up in piles against a broken fence
made up of old driftwood

the conversation moves away from what was done
over to what can be done about it all now
nobody wants to act like they can solve
a problem that has so many equations
unless they are allowed to cheat at
the math that gets the answer
wrong before the test is over

the thing that is there in love and not in rest
is the piece of the fence that gives way
letting the sand cover over the edge
in huge heaping dunes that swirl up
erasing any evidence that it was ever
there in first place

Length

he said, in obvious criticism:
'you write poems that are
too long, you lack editorial
talents and the self-control
it takes to write real modern
poetry that everyone can like,
that everyone can relate to,
frankly, I don't get it because
I don't read it, it is too long.'

I said, in polite reply:
'...I will eventually kill
everyone who will not
kill me first...'

we spoke no more
after that

Post-Modern Hyperreal Simulacra
Buckshot Poem

words shot through with lightening bolts of
provocation meeting words that subdue fantastic
dialectics head on render meaning from words
arranged like blood spatter at a murder scene that
has no victim until there is not
anymore balance in the thinking that is left reeling
on its own heel as it turns to make an exit strategy
until the primitive cultural bond is enacted upon its
final arch of uncivilized precursors to debates given
so long ago they have lost meaning like old punk
rock mix tapes made off of radio shows because
records were too hard for homeless kids to carry
into the street at night for their first attempt at
deconstructing every word that put emphasis on
conformity for the sake of identity that gets lost
across floors of abandoned hotels that no longer
figure into the scheme of economic viability
as numbers become compartments become lost
children become banned books and music and art
and fashion that became advertising and marketing
and cool that equated to dollar signs yen signs euro
signs gold standard never coming
back into solid credit futures shared with pork
bellied fraternity of future that really means past as
ticker tapes no longer inspire parades and
homelessness no longer inspires anger or humor just
how many more do we have to tolerate on our way
into the point of purchase as the money changers
become magnetic sliding devices on'
bar coded literary excesses of publish at any cost by
any means the shallowest memoirs, thinnest
political theories, grandest poetics

all hallow this without any god chosen above the commerce to worship as it is marketing and more marketing cleverness
like the first dadaist meant to stop wars, not help them conflagrate across the surface of the planet burning us all with grandiose promotional world tours that promote more bloodshed in the name of more healing as it politely asks
"well, how could you expect one without the other?"

la pistolera

he had given her a nickel plated .45
before he went to serve his time
she kept it in a velvet holster
between her silken thighs
all the while he was away
she kept it warm and oiled
always full of fresh ammo
a bullet in every chamber
she shot down many
of the interlopers
that would try to jump his claim
as if she was property to be taken
she always shot them true
the way her mama had taught her to aim
by the time he made it back to her
the years had peeled
so much of them both away
but, the pistol was immaculate
brighter than the day it was made
she put it firm into his hand
as together
they would finally
ride away

Stasis

The feeling is hard to shake sometimes.
Life in a holding pattern and no answer
from the ground control for clearance
to land.

The obvious sensation that something is
broken and the parts are no longer available
to make the necessary repairs so the
rust is the only progress being made.

Floating in the ether above the reality
of the world your mind will drift to all
sorts of far off places where you had
hoped to be, where you would have been
if it wasn't for that one thing, that snag in
the eternal plan that you tried to fix
oh so unsuccessfully.

I had a friend who was clever enough
to rig hiding places everywhere he lived
always perfecting his skills in case he might
return there with a need for what is hidden.

We had lived and fought to carve out
a life outside of the normal, daunting
world of the 9 to 5 hustlers that struck
fear into our hearts of a complacent death.

He always assured me that there was an
optimistic ending to this struggle, but I
had more experience evading the hands
of justice, a special knowledge that was
a bummer trip at most parties. So I mostly
 kept it to myself

I was smarter in that sense, my moves
likened more to chess, his more like a
game of checkers, even though he had
the flash and dazzle of personality.

It made his schemes seem bigger and more
fruitful than mine, but I could hear the keys
jingle on the correctional officers belt as they
walked past my cell every time he talked.

Still, I loved to hear how we were going to
increase our take in the business when he
would talk with well read words and the hand
gestures of a great magician.

It would sometimes calm my nerves and entertain
me on those days of waiting for the timing to be
right, for an opportunity that was artificially created
to open its scarcely seen maw wide enough to
behold a slight victory.

There is a dreariness to dealing drugs that is only
resolved with lots of money or a sense of stasis
achieved with a carefully calculated alcohol and
narcotic intake.
It is a painful dreariness that pinches the soul.

Because of this intensity in a sad pain
it is most difficult to achieve both goals in a
simultaneous way and maintain a cool enough
demeanor so as to not draw attention to the fact
that you are in over your head and a personal
Armageddon is imminent.

It grinds you down in the depth of your gut and
the money is useless unless it is spent immediately

and the building sadness becomes the elephant in the room that can no longer be ignored; the fear that life will never be normal is only countered by the reality that it never has been.

The clever friend did 5 years without snitching me out and when he was released I wanted to honor his time spent in stasis without his taking the short cut out, the rat way that I knew was the end for anyone. (If not for any reason other than they change into golems and cease to be real, I had encountered them many times and I had an affinity for smelling their stench and their nervous actions that gave them away.)

Bravado only goes so far as a cover against fear and tears have been more employed as manipulations in my realm of experience, but honest fear exposed to me is the only communication I can decipher into real meaning, and I saw it in his eyes that day.

After 5 years, mostly at Lompoc, he said he would never go back, he would not do it another time, as if to warn me, but I felt I had to honor that he was there because of this unwritten code that I was raised to live by and I dismissed it and I assured him if he was smarter and calmer this time around in his movements he would not have to go back, ever again.

But, somewhere deep inside my mind I knew I was marked, and I knew he couldn't stop playing checkers anymore than I could stop playing chess. So when the chips fell and I looked him in the eye for the last time, I asked him not to do the triple jump he had set up in front of us.

He shook my hand with a couple of crumpled
c-notes in it and smiled, reiterating that he could
not go back.

I never saw him again, like I have never seen any
of them again that walked away to that edge
dropping off into darkness, forever.

This last time I was put in chains, I was humbled
and beaten to the point that I wanted to do anything
to not go back to the chess pieces and the
motionless existence of kinetic movement in order
to be still.

In the institutional stasis again, silent for days,
reading, writing, thinking about how I could cut the
umbilical that connected me to the game and be
more connected to a life that I had never known,
a life I felt only mocked and scorned by.

You see, I was accomplished at a life in stasis with
subtle movement and calculated expectations that I
measured out over and over, but now I am clumsy
and uncertain as I plod this alien path and I know
bravado and tears won't do me any good.

Only love, the most fleeting and puzzling
experience I have ever known, has come close to
expediting my release and somehow the feeling of
the gun barrel in the guard tower that is aimed for
the back of my head is vanishing in its solvent.

Any slight misunderstanding of the implications of
love and I immediately crave the motionless stasis
and the cool darkened corners of artificial solitude
and the penalized sensation that I am not
responsible for the day.

I have not learned how to be that still while in love.

Everyday I am free now, seems to be another day of this lesson that I am learning. Love once held in stasis now must be set free.

The Art of Finding It Where You Can

in trying to put a life together
from broken sticks & gobs
of chewed stuff to keep
it together long enough
to make it into a shelter
things are found in the refuse
things are acquired from outside
the realm of the gutter that was home
for so long it was warm water on muddy cold days
everything comes down to the gutter
sooner or later
few things get up out of it
once they find a place here
& where you stay
& where you end up
is what your life can look like
from down here
all the way up there
or even if you are
on your way down again?
are you?
so sad, but
the gutter is always here to catch you
the broken sticks & gobs of chewed up stuff
are always plentiful
you see
up there, somewhere
someone keeps making more
& it seems to find its way down here
in larger & larger amounts

Together by the Campfire in Big Sur

glowing embers melting into this night's dark brow
like the tears of an obsidian ghost shadowing
granite canyon walls
washing into redwood memories
 of carbon dated love songs
soaking away with the smoke into
 the shoreline of stars
circled above the treetops so high
dissolved completely like foam
 in the undercurrent of the bay
that undulates in the distant tempo
 of a danger left behind

night looming above the treeline
 in a shooting star spectacle of hope
light ricocheting across the skies
 in defiance of all gravity
of all things grave, in this moment
air moving as cold wisps of coastal fog
in and out of lungs grateful for the breath,
even if it is the last
grateful, nonetheless

waterfalls surround in sounds
 that drown the drunken ocean
as it is crashing in the distance
 like a thousand drunken sailors
stumbling down a shanghai gangplank all at once

mothers and fathers of distortion
 are just a faint sound
easily drowned by the powerful volume
 of natural wonder

everyone present wants to forget
 the years lost at sea
including the salty ghosts of tremendous terror
that never found a home along this coastline
 of no safe harbor
or in the boggy marshes of deepest regret

two hearts know the truth they need to know
as the heat dwindles and the dew comes through
more readily
as the minds retreat into each other on purpose
seeking a final sanctified shelter from the world of
people

as if we have become a temporary cove
that we have both sought sanctuary in for this most
neutral of nights
in an oncoming spring
that has just begun to dance itself
 into a full swing symphony
playing silent strings in the echoing darkness
 of this loving forest
as it hugs two lovers closer to a bed
 of fallen twigs and needles
blanketing them with dreams
 of no modern consequence
so that they might sleep in the locked embrace
 of the living
forgetting the dying cities that they have
momentarily escaped
if only for this night next to a river running
 through coastal woods
along a rocky shoreline that keeps all fears at bay
while a half moon teardrop falls slowly
 to the ground

these embers sacrifice themselves into the living air
while sleeping lovers can dream of an awakening
into the hopeful renewal of an ever cleansing dawn

Trade

places are negotiable
to a point
then
no more

lives are interchangeable
in a way
but
not now
not like this

a sunrise
cannot be switched
with the smallest star

a broken heart
cannot replace
an open mind
full of hope

something gives
in the value
appraised
too low

something
does not
hold up
long
enough

walk away
empty handed
but never forget

what was lost
before you knew____you were losing it

El Finito

photo courtesy of Los Angeles Police Dept.

A. RAZOR was born in Brooklyn, N.Y. in 1963,
but was brought to California at the age of 1.
He was raised with a strong desire to read and write,
but an even greater desire to survive his
circumstances, which has aided his experience and
longevity so far. He began writing and publishing
around 1980 in various underground zines and
publications, first in the Los Angeles area, then
expanding outward after he was discovered by
Drew Blood Press, Ltd. in 1984.
He published 11 titles on that now defunct press
by 1995. He was not published again until 2012.
On January 13, 2012, he joined forces with Iris
Berry to create *Punk Hostage Press.*

Other Poetry/Prose Books by A. Razor –

Better Than A Gun In A Knife Fight (2012)
Drawn Blood: Collected Works, 1985-1995 (2012)
Small Catastrophes in A Big World (2012)

Titles edited by A. Razor –

FRACTURED, Danny Baker (2012)
The Daughters of Bastards, Iris Berry (2012)
impress, C.V. Auchterlonie (2012)
miracles of the BloG: A series,
　　Carolyn Srygley-Moore (2012)
8th & Agony, Rich Ferguson (2012)

Forthcoming Books by A. Razor –

Puro Purismo (poems) (2013)

Long Winded Tales of a
Low Plains Drifter (short stories) 2013

16302029R00122

Made in the USA
Charleston, SC
14 December 2012